Pets and the Afterlife 4

Rob Gutro

Pets and the Afterlife 4:
Messages from Spirit Cats

i

Cover: Cats crossing over the "Rainbow Bridge." By Getcovers.com, featuring images of Coco, Fudge and Gracie from stories within this book.

"Pets and the Afterlife 4," by Rob Gutro. ISBN-13: 9798353524366

###

Books by Rob Gutro

Pets and the Afterlife Series:
- Pets and the Afterlife 1: How they communicate from the other side and more
- Pets and the Afterlife 2: Stories of signs from pets that passed
- Pets and the Afterlife 3: Messages from Spirit Dogs
- Pets and the Afterlife 4: Messages from Spirit Cats

Ghosts and Spirits Series:
- Case Files of Inspired Ghost Tracking
- Kindred Spirits: How a Medium Befriended a Spirit
- Lessons Learned from Talking to the Dead
- Ghosts and Spirits: Explained

On a Medium's Vacation Series:
- Ghosts of England on a Medium's Vacation
- Ghosts of the Bird Cage Theatre on a Medium's Vacation

Dedication

This book is dedicated to all of the animal rescues I've been fortunate to work with, including: Adirondack Save A Stray, NY; Animal Rescue League of NH, Bedford, NH; Animal Rescue of Rhode Island, Wakefield, RI; Coast to Coast Dachshund Rescue, NJ; Dachshund Rescue of North America, NJ; DC Area Weimaraner Rescue, Washington, D.C.; Humane Society of Calvert County, Sunderland, MD; Just One More Dachshund Rescue, Huntingtown, MD; Knick Knack Pittie Pack Rescue, Mont Alto, PA; Lakes Region Humane Society, Ossipee, NH; Long Dogs and Friends Rescue, PA: Northeast Animal Shelter, Salem, MA, Pet ResQ, Tenafly, NJ; Prince George's County Animal Shelter, MD; Sophia's Grace Foundation, PA; (the former) Wolf Creek Weimaraner Rescue, TN; Yorkie 911 Rescue, NY and more.

The experiences in this book are true. Some names have been changed to protect the privacy of the individual providing the story at their request.

I wrote this book to help pet parents in their time of grief over the loss of their beloved cats. Pets of all types are members of our family and dealing with their loss is very real and a significant life event.

My deepest appreciation to all who work with animal rescues, in kennels, shelters, and in veterinary medicine for the unconditional love they give to these wonderful animals.

Contents

Preface

Welcome to the fourth volume of *Pets and the Afterlife*. This book focuses entirely on the many ways cats in spirit communicate they are still around in the afterlife.

This book differs from the previous three *Pets and the Afterlife* books because it is solely about messages from cats in spirit. Like *Pets and the Afterlife 3: Messages from Spirit Dogs*, it also directly addresses feelings of loss and grief and offers ways to work through them. In preparing this book, I consulted with a licensed clinical social worker who graciously donated her experience, time, and insight so that you may understand how to work through your grief.

Like the previous books in this series, *Pets and the Afterlife 4* provides examples describing the many ways our pets can communicate from the other side through personal stories. It is through these stories that I hope you will find comfort by understanding how your pets are communicating with you from the other side.

If you are reading this book, you have probably lost a best friend, a confidante, and a part of yourself from the passing of your beloved pet. I understand these feelings as I have also experienced them, and I am truly sorry for your loss.

You will read about messages that I received from pets and the confirmations provided by their pet parents. In addition, you will read about the experiences of other pet parents who picked up on the messages from their pets who passed.

After reading this book, it is my hope you will come to realize our departed pets are still with us. They can hear our words and our thoughts even though they may not be with us in the physical plane.

Keep an open mind as you read this book. We all have a lot to learn about this life and the next. Many of the occurrences we may be quick to dismiss might actually be a sign from a spirit (a loved one who crossed over) attempting to communicate with us. One thing you will learn is that there is no such thing as a coincidence when it comes to spirits.

We also need to be cautious. Not everything is a sign from a spirit. I wrote this book and the previous books in the series so you will begin to learn how to discern what may be a message of love for you.

I use my gift to help others when I can. I do provide short pet spirit readings for a small fee, and details are available on my website.

If you would like a personal email reading for your cat in spirit, please visit my website for details at: www.robgutro.com. Please keep in mind that I am booked in advance, so I appreciate your patience.

For an in-depth personal reading for a human spirit, I recommend Ruthie Larkin, the Beantown Medium at www.Beantownmedium.com.

I am available for lectures and speaking engagements. I have given many talks about pets and the afterlife as fundraisers for animal rescues. If you know of an animal rescue that would be interested in having me do a fundraising lecture, please contact me through email or my website.

If you have questions or stories you would like to share, please write to me at Rgutro@gmail.com, or via my website or social media sites.

Websites: www.robgutro.com or www.petspirits.com
(The above links go to the same place)
Facebook:
https://www.facebook.com/RobGutroAuthorMedium
https://www.facebook.com/ghostsandspirits.insightsfromame
dium
Instagram: https://www.instagram.com/robgutro_author/
Amazon Author Page: amazon.com/author/robgutro
YouTube:
https://tinyurl.com/wcvhqbt

I look forward to hearing from you and wish you peace and comfort knowing that our pets' love binds us to them "fur-ever."

Rob Gutro

Introduction

This book is comprised of two parts.

The first part is "Understanding and Coping with Loss and Grief." It is written in part by a professional who counsels people through grief. You'll also read how I dealt with the passing of two of our dogs which may help you.

The second part is "Stories of Pet Spirit Communications." It is arranged alphabetically by each cat's name. It includes messages I have received from passed pets who wanted to communicate with their pet parents and experiences that other pet parents have shared with me of their encounters.

After reading this book, it is my hope that you can more easily work through your grief by understanding that your pets are still with you. You'll learn of their signs and recognize their attempts to communicate with you.

My Lifetime Experiences with Pets
During my childhood my parents adopted two dogs. I immediately developed a love and affinity for them. Although young, I recognized the unconditional love they unselfishly gave.

Our first family dog, Penny, a Cocker Spaniel, passed when I was four years old, and it was traumatic. In fact, it's the earliest memory I have as a child. I don't remember Penny, but at 4 years old I recall my mother crying on the phone with the veterinarian who told her there was no choice but to put Penny "to sleep." I've never forgotten that feeling of grief and the sense of loss.

Years later, my parents adopted a toy poodle. My mother named her Gigi. I remember Gigi had a broken leg and my mom nursed her back to full health.

I loved Gigi and would talk to her about everything. I considered her a best friend and a confidante although she was really bonded to my mom.

In 1993, when I was on a work detail in Miami, I remember the phone call from my parents in Boston when they told me Gigi passed at 18 years old. Although I hadn't seen Gigi in months since my last visit home, our love had forged a strong bond and I cried on the phone with my mom. That grief and sense of loss stayed with me a long time.

Today, I half-joke that my mother loved her dogs more than she loved her three boys. However, there's some truth to that!

Today, my husband and I are the proud "dog parents" to a dachshund and two dachshund-chihuahua mixes. We have been working with dog rescues since 2009 and have done transports, fostering, home visits, website work, promotions, events, and fundraising.

Dogs and cats hold a special place in my life and my heart as I am sure they do for you if you are reading this book.

###

PART 1: Understanding and Coping with Loss and Grief

Chapter 1
Why Pet Passings are Devastating

When a pet companion passes, the sense of loss can be emotionally and mentally crippling to us. I know. I've lost four precious dogs: three to old age and another as a puppy in a horrible accident. In this brief chapter, I explain why the sense of loss is so deep.

Whenever I give lectures on how pets communicate from the afterlife, I explain the deep sense of loss using scientific studies (because, well, I'm a scientist).

It is scientifically proven that our cats and dogs have the intelligence of a 3-to-5-year-old human child. In my previous books on pets and the afterlife, I cited those studies. Another scientific study showed that pets love the same way that people do, except pets don't love with conditions. The love a pet gives is truly unconditional and therefore deeper than our capability as humans.

Given those studies and the understanding that pets will always behave like 3-to-5-year-old children even as they age into teenage human years (which are elderly years by cat or dog standards), we still look at them as those young children.

As a result, when they pass, even at 14 or 15 years of age, in our minds they are still 3-to-5-year-olds (human children equivalents). As adults we know that children should never outlive their parents. *But because they are cats and dogs their lifespan is different and shorter. Even though we are aware of that, we still perceive our pets as young children.*

That's why we grieve so deeply for our pets. They are, in essence, children who age physically, but stay the same in terms of behavior and unconditional love (unlike people).

The Extremes

Since publishing my first *Pets and the Afterlife* book, I have received thousands of emails from people around the world asking for a sign from their spirit pets. Several people have also told me they were suicidal and could not go on without their pet in the physical world. I assured them their pet is with them in spirit, and their pet wants them to live full lives.

Although I understand the deep, painful sense of loss, I'm not a counselor or a therapist. That said, I can only convey messages from pets and people who passed away. If you or someone you know has those suicidal feelings, please call the U.S. National Suicide Prevention Lifeline at 1-800-273-8255 or dial 988. If you're reading this from another country, please look up the number on the Internet and dial it if you need it.

What Our Pets Want Us to Know

If you or someone you know is hurting that deeply or feels that way, you need to know our pets in spirit want us to never go to that extreme. Our pets acknowledge the love they felt for their parent still exists after they become a spirit.

They want us to live our lives and take the love we provided them and give it to another animal who may otherwise not have a chance at experiencing love and a good home.

For anyone experiencing deep grief, this book provides you with information about the ways your pets will try and communicate with you from spirit, so your grief and pain ease by knowing they'll always be tied to you. In fact, our pets will be waiting in the light for us whenever it is our time.

###

Chapter 2
Experiencing Loss in Different Ways

Dealing with the death of a pet is traumatic, whether it is watching a slow decline or a tragic accident; my dogs passed in both ways. Although an accidental death may be more jarring to the pet parent, any way in which a beloved pet passes is emotionally traumatic.

In teaching you how cats communicate with the living, it is my hope that once you recognize a sign, it will provide some comfort and help you better navigate through your grief.

(Photo: Baldrick and Mrs. Miggins, from Pets and the Afterlife book 2. Credit: Vittoria Conn)

Some passings occur quickly or suddenly. In the <u>first two *Pets and the Afterlife* books</u> I shared that my dog Buzz passed as a 7-month-old puppy when he was tragically killed by a speeding car. I also shared how our dachshund mix, Sprite, passed at 16 years old from declining health and a tumor that burst inside his nose.

Other pets experience illnesses that continue over time. Cats may battle cancer, Feline HIV, seizures, heart issues or arthritis. Caring for a cat when they face illnesses like these over time may emotionally prepare us better for their passing, but when they pass, the empty feeling is still there.

Feelings of Guilt

Grief is also sometimes accompanied by guilt. Sometimes we feel guilty for thinking we didn't do enough or there was something we should have done differently. We may wonder if we let them go too early, or if we held on too long. I experienced both of those feelings with our dog Franklin, whom you can read about Pets and the Afterlife 3.

I suffered from intense guilt immediately after Buzz's passing from the car accident. I kept thinking that I never should have walked him that way on that day (afterward in spirit, Buzz told me it was his time). I felt guilty, responsible, lost, and empty. I felt as if I failed him. But I could never have known there would be a dog across the street that would cause him to pull, and I certainly didn't expect a speeding car on a quiet street. I cried myself to sleep many nights holding his toys, and over a short time, that pain eased as I recognized signs from him.

Buzz made me realize his short life served several larger purposes. He taught me what unconditional love meant. That's a great gift no matter how long or short a time we experience it. That's what your cat has done for you.

Through his messages, Buzz taught me how pets communicate from the other side. Knowing this, I have been able to help comfort other grieving pet parents.

Buzz also opened the "spiritual door" that allowed me to communicate with domesticated animals in the afterlife.

Sprite's condition required making the decision to euthanize him and help him out of pain. It's natural to question that decision repeatedly. After Sprite passed, I came home and hugged our other dogs and cried. I felt guilt. I felt like I failed him. Going over his medical conditions and recalling the emergency vet citing the burst nasal tumor was a call to let Sprite pass in peace. I realized it was right for Sprite and that's what was most important. So, go over the facts. You'll find it reassuring and it will lessen guilty feelings.

Remember, it takes a tremendous amount of unconditional love to help someone we love to pass.

I realized at these times, there will always be things we don't know, and we must do our best. It's all we can do. We do it out of love. Our cats can't speak to us, but we can pay attention to them and observe their body language and behavior to get a clue about how they are feeling physically and mentally.

Our pets don't want us to feel guilty for helping them cross when they're in pain. I get many, many messages from cats and dogs in spirit who thank their pet parents for having the courage to allow them to pass out of pain.

The Emptiness Hurts
When our Dachshund, Franklin passed in May 2020, I noted that the physical loss of our boy had been traumatic for us. We have the memories... but his bed was empty. We've had to say goodbye to a best friend and a child. We hug our other kids a lot. We put his bed away to help alleviate the sense of

loss. If it helps you, you should do it, too. You can also donate things to a rescue in your cat's memory.

Remember the Good Things

Remember the good things in your cat's life. Don't focus on the loss and emptiness. Look at photos of your pets. Recall the good days, the bad days, and the lazy or active days. Photos are also helpful in providing visual clues that show a cat's decline over time, since we don't see that while living with them on a day-to-day basis.

No matter in what manner your pet passes, it's usually going to be emotionally devastating. Keep in mind that they love us and are grateful for the love we shared with them. There is no need for guilt. It's all about love.

###

Chapter 3
A Professional's Advice to Cope With Grief

The sense of loss can be mentally and emotionally crippling. Sometimes it's not enough to understand how pets still communicate with us from the afterlife. Although that understanding provides comfort, we still must deal with our own emotions of grief. In this chapter you'll learn ways to cope with and reduce the intensity of that grief.

Over my years of communicating with pet parents about their struggles with grief and loss, I've read about the range of emotions they've suffered. Some were depressed and even suicidal. Others were struggling with feelings of guilt and remorse. One person felt anger by the loss of her pet and directed it toward me for not immediately responding to her email. I understand these emotions and have experienced them myself as I have lost four beautiful canine children.

To work through these emotions and times of grief, I reached out to my good friend Kristin Young, LICSW MSW, who has been a Clinical Social Worker in the state of Massachusetts, and who has worked in the field of mental health and addictive disorders for nearly 20 years.

***

Kristin provided the following insight on how to address your grief and work through it:

Over the last 20 years of working in the field of mental health and addiction, I have seen many people through grief and loss. It is always difficult to understand and move through the emotions related to the loss of a loved one, and many people are not prepared for the intensity of the grief surrounding the loss of a beloved pet. Some even find it more difficult to cope with pet loss.

I believe this is due to a few different factors: First, we must care for pets in similar ways to caring for children, so many of us end up with bonds that may mimic those of a parent and a child. Even though logically we understand the difference, and we may be fully aware of differences in life expectancy, our hearts don't always understand that logic. Thus, we are left with feelings like that of losing a child, but an intellect that says otherwise. This creates more confusion and adds to the complexity of the grief.

Second, our society often does not validate our grief in the same way as with the loss of a human loved one. We aren't afforded time off from work, there isn't a formalized way to say goodbye, and our friends and family members are typically not wrapping themselves around us with love and bringing casseroles, thus leaving many of us in a lonelier unvalidated form of grief.

Third, we are faced with constant reminders of the loss and the very large void left behind. As our pets loved us unconditionally for years, they would always be there to greet us excitedly. After their passing, home can become a very difficult place to be.

Now that we understand a little bit about why the loss of a pet can be so traumatic, let's talk about how we can better learn to cope. First, I'd like to quickly mention the 5 stages of grief according to The Kubler Ross model. This is just a guide, and not at all a rule. Some people do not experience all 5 stages, many experience all the stages but not in this order, and some will move in and out of a few over time. If you are or have experienced any of these stages, please know that they are all completely normal when grieving.

The five stages are:
- **Denial**: Doubting the reality of the loss. Some may even fantasize about it being a mistake, and that the beloved pet will be back at any moment.
- **Anger**: Pain from a loss is often redirected as anger. This anger may be directed at other people, places, and even objects.
- **Bargaining**: This is an internal negotiation with "what ifs" or "If onlys." For example: "If I had only done *this* instead of *that* everything would still be okay."
- **Depression**: This is just sadness and is completely normal when we are experiencing loss.
- **Acceptance**: In this stage we have come to accept, and have learned how to live with, the loss.

So, how do we get through all of this? Sometimes it can feel as if the sadness will consume us. I promise it won't. Try and remind yourself that this awful heaviness will not be there forever. It will eventually dissipate, but that will take time. How much time will be different for everyone. There is no timeline on grief and try to allow yourself or your loved one to just be where you/they are with no judgement. In the meantime, here are some things you can do to help:

- **Plan Distractions:** Do things. Things that bring you joy, things that need to get done, things that you have been putting off. Your brain needs some space from the heavy and sad thoughts. Take that space.

- **Start a new tradition:** Do something new in honor or your beloved pet. Maybe you donate to a rescue mission in your beloved pets name once or twice a year, or create a special tribute to your pet and spend some time reflecting on your life together? Honoring your time together in some way can help bring a sense of peace.

- **Stay Connected:** Stay connected to the world around you. Don't isolate for long periods of time, even when it's hard. Move towards people who validate your grief, and away from those who don't. There will be plenty of time for everyone once you're feeling better.

- **Take some space:** I know I just said to stay connected, but it is also necessary to sometimes take some space. You need to sit in the grief and just feel it sometimes. It's okay to cry. That is our body's way of getting out the sadness. Just don't stay here for days. Try and have a healthy combination of connection and space.

- **Take care of yourself:** This is where the catch phrase "self-care" comes up. What does that mean? It means to do the things that keep you well. For most of us that is sleeping (even if it is fragmented from the grief), eating nutritious food, staying away from excessive amounts of alcohol (it makes things worse in the long run), moving your body daily, and some form of mindfulness or meditation. Just sitting and talking out loud to your beloved pet can be a form of self-care. I do believe they can hear you. If you don't believe that yet, you will after finishing this book.

- **Keep a schedule:** Keeping a regular schedule can help you feel more productive, which gives us all a boost. It also helps with distractions.

- **Don't put a time limit on grief:** As mentioned earlier, there is no time limit on grief, nor is there a "normal" amount of time to be sad. Putting pressure on yourself to get over it will only make things worse. That leads to self judgement and more depression. Wherever you are in your journey is exactly where you should be. Having said that, if you feel like you're not getting any better or are having thoughts of harming yourself in anyway please reach out for help…

- **Consider counseling:** Counselors are trained to help in times like this. We have tools we can teach you that have science backing them. They are proven to help grieving people feel better.

- **NEVER LOSE HOPE:** Things will get better

***

About Kristin Young:

Kristin Young, LICSW MSW has been a Clinical Social Worker in the state of Massachusetts since 2009. She is currently the Clinical Director of Herren Project, and also has a private practice on Cape Cod. She holds a Master's Degree in Clinical Social Work from Boston University School of Social Work, a Bachelor's in Neuroscience from Smith College, and has worked in the field of mental health and addictive disorders for nearly 20 years. Kristin has worked with individuals with chronic and severe mental health issues and co-occurring disorders and has served in mental health centers and recovery residences. She has a specialty in addiction and recovery, trauma, and chronic mental health issues.

***

Rob's Suggestions to Help Cope with Loss

Confirming the Decision Without Guilt

One of the most common feelings we experience is a feeling of guilt after helping our pet pass out of pain. I know I have felt that way. But it's a guilt that we should not have, because we helped our pets out of pain. It's easy to say we shouldn't feel guilty, but that doesn't make it better.

I found two ways that helped me understand that I made the right decision. Hopefully, they will help you, too:

1. Email a friend about your cat's declining health - In a method similar to the journaling, I emailed a friend and listed all the health conditions my dog Sprite was experiencing before he passed, that led me to the decision. My friend emailed me back my own email and said "Read this as if someone else was telling you about their dog and their decision. Then tell me if you did the right thing." I did, and it made me realize I did the right thing.

2. Look at a timeline of photos - After our dog Franklin passed in May 2020, we continued to doubt ourselves and wonder if we made the right decision. One thing we did was to look at photos of Franklin over the last year of his life, leading up to the day we had to help him cross over out of pain.

We noticed his posture became increasingly worse, which can be attributed to a slipped disc getting progressively worse. We noticed how much he had physically aged in that year. The photos were mostly of Franklin in a bed because he no longer walked around.

Making that fateful decision for our pets requires the greatest level of love and compassion we can have for another living thing.

When we love someone, we don't want to see them suffer at the end of their lives. We want them to pass with peace and dignity. As caregivers to our pets, it's our responsibility to do what is best for them. That requires a lot of courage.

It's also important to understand that our pets know the emotional turmoil we endure trying to make that decision. They can read our energy, just as they sense what mood we're in. They also appreciate the courage and love it takes to help them find peace at the end of their time here in the physical world. Knowing that, they also don't want us to feel guilt. Instead, they are grateful.

###

Chapter 4
Ways We Coped with Grief and Loss

Everyone grieves differently. I've learned that by talking with a lot of people who have lost pets and people. There's no set timeline to get past your grief. This chapter contains some of the things that helped me work through my grief.

One source of comfort is understanding your pet is in spirit and they will visit you from time to time. There are things you can do around your house to help cope. Here are some ideas:

My friend Jackie suggested **creating a memorial garden if you have a yard**. If you don't have a yard, create a memorial spot in your home. Jackie sent us a memorial plaque which we placed outside with plaques we made for our dogs who passed. **Plant colorful flowers** to create good feelings.

We received **beautiful paintings** of Franklin and Dolly from our friends Michael and Bryan. You can commission paintings online (it's affordable) by sending companies a photograph.

Reading cards and well-wishes from friends is very healing. If you **post something on social media,** it gives many people an opportunity to comment. There's nothing more healing than hearing from family, friends and acquaintances who can sympathize or relate in some way.

Poetry and music are other outlets to channel the loss into a positive memory. Write a poem, lyrics or compose music about your pet. It's a nice way to honor them. Michael and Darci sent us a book of poems about dogs.

My brother and his girlfriend sent us **memorial wind chimes**. Every time the wind blows, and we hear the chimes, we know Franklin and Dolly are nearby in spirit.

Donate to a cat rescue in memory of your pet. I encourage memorial rescue donations to help living cats. As a dog rescue volunteer, I highly recommend doing this.

If you have your cat's ashes create a spot for them where you can see them daily. Place a photo next to them. It's perfectly fine to talk with your pet in spirit looking at their box of ashes. Remember they are not in there. They are around you and they can hear your voice and your thoughts. Both sound and thoughts are energy, and as beings of energy they can hear you. It does help us when we talk with people and pets who have passed. It's all part of the healing process.

###

Chapter 5
Q&A About People and Pets who Grieve

This chapter contains questions that readers of my books have asked me about grief, loss, and acceptance. The first part of this chapter is questions related to grief experienced by pet parents.

Q: What advice would you give someone who can't seem to grapple with the loss of a pet or find closure?

A: Know that your pets in spirit are around you. Close your eyes and know that the love we share binds us together forever. Love is an amazing energy and energy can't be destroyed. Keep your mind open, too. Don't discount anything that may be a sign because there's no such thing as a coincidence when it comes to spirit.

Pets, like people who pass, don't want us to be stuck in grief. Although grieving is a natural part of experiencing physical loss, it should not cripple you and prevent you from enjoying life and love. Our late pets (and people) want us to be happy, and live our lives, and to help other pets who don't have homes or the love that our late pets enjoyed. One of the best ways to pay tribute to a pet that passed is to adopt or foster another and give that pet a chance to experience love (and not waste the love you have to give).

Q: What's one of the most memorable moments you've had or felt while connecting with one of your dogs in the afterlife?

A: After my late dachshund Sprite passed in 2013, he sent us a butterfly. Spirits have the ability to manipulate and influence things in nature, like birds, butterflies, feathers, flowers, etc.

All summer long, we hadn't seen a butterfly in our backyard, despite having two butterfly bushes. However, after Sprite's passing when we let our other three dogs out in the backyard, a large yellow and black butterfly flew around them for quite a long time and they didn't chase after it (usually they would). The butterfly landed on the grass near them and sat (I took several close-up photos of it). The dogs walked around it, as if they were walking around Sprite. We knew Sprite sent the butterfly.

Two of my friends in other states also had encounters with Sprite's butterfly because the timing was perfect. You can read the full story in Pets and the Afterlife 1.

Q: Why do only some pets come through or send signs while other don't?

A: It all depends on the pet's personality. Pets who were shy or quiet in life, tend to be the same in the afterlife, and they often let the more "social" pets do the talking, just as people do.

Usually, once a pet comes through and knows the pet parent understands they are okay in spirit, they will not continue to come through as often as they did right after their passing.

Q: What would you tell someone who is desperately trying to reach their pet on the other side to no avail?

A: Pets, like people, only come through with signs when they have something to tell us. People and pets usually return around the times of birthdays, anniversaries, or holidays, too -either theirs or ours. They all give us signs - we just miss them, which is why I wrote the books to educate people on how to see them!

Q: If I'm deep in grief, will I be able to see my pet's signs?

A: Grief blocks out signs. When we are grieving and desperate to see something, it's harder to acknowledge a sign and we tend to dismiss things for something more "concrete."

Sometimes if a pet can't get through to a parent, they'll come through to someone else in the family, or someone who knows the pet parent. Examples would be if one person in the family, or a friend of yours dreams of your cat who passed, but you can't dream of him/her. That means that your cat had to go to someone they know would convey the dream to you, so you would know they are okay in spirit.

If you are overwhelmed with grief, talk with a counselor to help lessen the grief (so your pets can come through), or you can even go to a medium.

***

The rest of this chapter is devoted to questions and answers about pets grieving for other pets.

In my other books in the "Pets and the Afterlife" series, I provided scientific proof that animals, mammals, etc. all have the same emotions humans have. If you have a couple of dogs or cats and one passes, the living animals will grieve as intensely as you do.

Q: Do Pets Grieve Other Pets?

A: Yes. Absolutely. Cats and dogs and other animals experience the same feelings of loss, sadness, and emptiness that humans experience when a loved one dies.

Q: I've heard other mediums say that pets don't really notice the passing of each other because they know the deceased is still present in spirit form. Is that your experience?

A: No. That's not my experience at all. Cats and dogs have the intelligence of a 3-to-5-year-old child. Animals in the wild even know when one of their pack has died.

Yes, pets can indeed see spirits. However, they know that a spirit is not a living, breathing animal, because there is usually no scent with the spirit. It takes a lot of energy for spirit to simply be visible. It would take a tremendous amount of energy to also mimic their scent. So, animals know the difference between a living animal and a ghost or spirit.

Q: I've had pets who really bonded with each other and when one of them passed the other seemed to grieve quite extensively. In one case, it was nearly three months before one of my cats seemed to get over his feelings of intense grief. In another instance, one of my cats died, and her buddy, also a cat, wouldn't eat for days and only slept in her spot.

A: Bonded pets are much more susceptible to grief than a non-bonded pair. Bonded pairs experience the same intense grief that humans do when their life-long partner passes. They behave the same way humans do, they are depressed, don't eat, find it hard to sleep, are restless and sad.

When our dog Franklin passed in 2020, our Weimaraner, Dolly and our other Dachshund, Tyler, understood what happened and behaved in a very subdued manner for quite some time.

Q: When my parents' dog was killed by another dog, their cats spent weeks looking for him. They never saw his body after he passed because he was taken to the vet hospital.

A: When one pet dies, it helps to have the living pets present (if possible) to understand that the other pet passed. Think of it this way. If you are a deaf human child of 4 or 5 years old and don't understand hand signals, and your father rushes your mother out the door, and your mother passes at the hospital - you have no idea why your mom never came back.

You get irritated, sad, depressed, worried. It's the same kind of thing a dog or cat experiences. As I wrote in my Pets and the Afterlife 1 book, when my dog Buzz died after being struck by a car, my roommate's dog (whom I was also walking) went over and sniffed him. He then understood that Buzz had passed. When he returned home, he picked up Buzz's favorite toy and kept it next to him, despite never having played with a toy throughout his entire 7 years). That dog showed that he was grieving the loss of Buzz's life.

Q: We are currently dealing with the impending death of one of our kitties due to cancer. He has begun refusing his medication, so in keeping with what I believe are his wishes, I've stopped giving them. He has a buddy, too. Can you explain how the after-death communications (ADCs) work for pets?

A: Pets can appear in spirit immediately after they pass. When your cat passes, your other cat or dog will see the spirit cat whenever they visit. If the living cat or dog is in the presence of your cat as he/she passes, they will understand what has happened.

Q: Do all animals experience grief and loss?

A: Yes. All domesticated and wild animals experience grief and loss.

In August 2018 a female orca whale named Tahlequa gave birth to a stillborn calf, and in her grief, she carried the baby around for 2 weeks. Various news outlets including National Geographic and CNN reported that Tahlequah finally released her dead calf's body after carrying it around the Pacific Northwest's waters for 17 days. She was grieving.

In a CNN article, Michael Milstein of the National Oceanic and Atmospheric Administration's West Coast Region was quoted as saying, "This kind of behavior is like a period of mourning and has been seen before. What's extraordinary about this is the length of time."

Marine biologists believed Tahlequah did not want her calf's body to sink to the ocean floor. So, she nudged it toward the surface as she swam through the Pacific Ocean.

Scientists say that grieving is common among mammals. Scientists have recorded symptoms of grieving among mammals such as elephants, deer, whales, and dolphins.

###

Chapter 6
Time, Transition, Intelligence & Signs

This chapter provides an abbreviated look at how cats indicate they want to pass, what happens to a pet's soul after they pass, the difference between spirits and ghosts, and it gives a quick overview of their intelligence and how they communicate.

Pets Know When It is Time
Pets will let you know when they are too tired to continue. In my *Pets 2 book* there is an entire chapter dedicated to when pets signal they know it's their time. For brevity's sake, know that when they stop eating or isolate themselves from you, those are some signs they are failing and ready to go.

Cats and dogs also get frustrated with themselves when they find they cannot do simple tasks like getting out of bed. Over time, if they struggle to walk because of advanced arthritis, they may lose their will to try anymore.

Pets may also isolate themselves from the parents. In 2020, our Dachshund, Franklin insisted on being by himself at the end when he was sickly. Because he had mobility issues, we would carry him in a room with us after dinner. In his 16 ½ years he always stayed with us in the room. But near the end of his life, he managed to get up and struggled to walk out of the room and drag himself in the kitchen to be alone. We knew it was time.

Stay With Them at the End
If you are euthanizing your pet, find the strength to stay with them during the process. They counted on you during their time here, and they don't want to see a stranger as they pass. They want to see you. If you don't have the emotional

strength, leave with the vet a piece of clothing with your scent on it so they can think you're there as they fade. No one wants to die alone unless they choose to do so by wandering off around your home. Try to get a sense of whether they want to pass with you there or without you. If they were isolating from you in the days before they are euthanized, then they likely would be okay with crossing alone.

More often than not, pets prefer someone with them.
Imagine what it would feel like when it's your time. Would you want to be alone or in the presence of someone you love?

The Capability to Communicate
Pets and the Afterlife 1, 2 and 3 go into detail about the different levels of learning that our pets experience, their intelligence and their emotions. Each of those books also describe the scientific studies that prove our pets have the intelligence of 3-to-5-year-old human children and the same emotions as humans. Because our pets possess that level of intelligence, we know that's how they can communicate with the living.

The Intelligence of Cats
Cats are intelligent enough to communicate with us from the other side after they've passed, just as they do in the physical.

In the first volume of "Pets and the Afterlife" I discussed the different levels of learning development in dogs, but the same applies to cats. Dr. Stanley Coren, DVM, published several books describing in depth the characteristics of each level which include language and gestures, game playing, instinctual intelligence, emotional intelligence, loyalty, a daily routine, recognition of locations, different barks (or meows) and body language, and facial signals. Dr. Coren's research showed that dogs possess the intelligence of a 3-to-5-year-old child and cats have a similar intelligence.

Another researcher on the topic, Temple Grandin, likened the intelligence in dogs to that of an autistic child. This would likely also apply to cats.

Once I read Temple Grandin's *Animals in Translation*, I was able to decipher what was scaring my Weimaraner, Dolly, whenever I let her out in our fenced in backyard. After reading the book, I investigated the backyard in search of anything that could be identified as the source of Dolly's fear. My investigation revealed that an unstrapped silver-colored grill cover that sometimes caught the wind. After removing the grill cover, Dolly was no longer afraid of going outside. I just had to see the world as she saw it.

Dr. Coren noted that dogs have different barks, just as cats have different meows, and purrs. There are those of happiness, alarm, or irritation. So, cat spirits can use those same verbal sounds to communicate from the other side.

A 2022 Study About Cat and Name Recognition
In April 2022, the peer-reviewed journal Scientific Reports published an article from scientists at Kyoto University who found that cats living with other feline friends can recognize their own and each other's names, and possibly even familiar humans' names.

During the experiment, researchers let cats hear humans call names of other cats in the same household. The images of named cats and others were then displayed on a monitor to examine their reaction. The results showed that the cats kept looking at the photos of unnamed cats longer, suggesting they know the names of the other cats in their home. In addition, researchers tested if domestic cats can distinguish various human family members. The study found that cats from larger households often stared longer at the faces of unnamed people.

This is not a surprise to me, as for years, cats in spirit have been providing me with their names and names of loved ones, both animal and human, on the other side.

Now that we know how they are capable of conveying messages, I will examine what happens when their physical bodies pass.

Soul 101: What Is a Soul?
All living things have a soul: humans, animals, and plants. Science has even documented that plants "scream" when being cut or killed. The collective energies of every living thing can be considered a part of the "god energy" or an energy source of light.

At the point of physical death, the energy that propels an earthbound body combines with the soul – memories, knowledge and personality of the living being (whether human or animal). As energy we make a choice: depart this Earthly plane and join the multitude of other energies that run through the universe as a "spirit," or stay here on Earth as a "ghost."

Of course, animals have souls. They have emotions, intelligence, and personalities of their own. After all, what makes one animal a pack leader and not all of them? Why are some animals shy? Why are some animals easily frightened, while others are bold?

In my experience, about 95 percent of animals cross over. That means they become spirits and join the energies of the "other side," "Heaven," etc. with our human loved ones.

The other five percent who don't opt to cross over and choose to stay earthbound in a fixed location of their choosing are those I call "ghosts." Ghosts stay behind for various reasons. Some love where they lived, others are afraid to cross over. Some think they can help their loved ones through grief (which they can't as a ghost). There are a multitude of reasons why people and animals can choose to stay earthbound because we all have our own personalities.

It's all About Energy
Both ghosts and spirits use energy to get strong enough to communicate with the living. In my Pets books, I describe energy in detail. For this book, I want to remind readers that spirits who crossed over (like our pets) use physical energies like heat, light, water and electricity, and emotional energies like love, faith, and hope. Earthbound ghosts draw on negative emotional energy like fear, anxiety, and anger.

Every action a spirit takes, like making a noise, meowing, purring out loud or entering our dreams requires using their energy. So, after they give a sign, their energy level must be replenished before they are capable of giving another sign.

Knowing this, you should also be able to understand that's why spirits can't come to us every single day. It takes the buildup of energy over time for spirit to get strong enough to convey their presence. So be patient!

Some Ways Pets Communicate from Spirit

Pay attention around anniversaries of significant events, birthdays, and holidays. Anniversaries can be adoption or passing dates. Human and animal spirits always acknowledge those dates and come around.

Think of the ways that cats communicate with you in the physical world. They make noises. You may hear a collar jingle, light footsteps on the stairs, or a meow (which, in spirit, always sounds like it's coming from another room). They can move things, make you feel them (often curled up sleeping against you), put impressions of paw prints on rugs, towels, beds, etc., lead you to another pet that looks like them, generate certain odors (like kitty litter or their favorite food scent), come into your dreams, influence living creatures like insects and birds to act oddly on certain dates, and many other ways.

Signs May Be Based on Life Experiences

Every cat will decide which method they use to communicate their presence based on their own life experiences.

You might feel a slight heaviness on your feet when you sit at the kitchen table, if they would position themselves there when they were physically here. You may feel their paw brush your hair in bed when your head is on your pillow. Cats are creatures of habit. They behave in spirit as they did when they were alive.

That's not to say they can't give other signs like manipulating birds or butterflies to behave erratically on special dates associated with you or them. Further, I'm not saying that every bird or butterfly is a sign; they have to act oddly within a 2-week window of a special date associated with your cat.

They can also give you certain numbers, dates, or names. They can leave you coins with the year of their birth, adoption or passing. But they do those things with the help of human spirits on the other side.

A Caution About Looking for Signs

Remember that not everything is a sign. It's easy to get carried away and think everything is a sign. It takes energy for spirit to give us signs, so they won't be leaving them every day. It's too exhausting for them. Once you acknowledge a message and their occasional presence the messages will only come when they think you need to hear from them. Visits are usually associated with a date or time relevant to them or you.

Some Things Pets Have Communicated to Me

Our human relatives in spirit often guide our pets to the other side. One spirit dog described to me his mom's father (the dog's grandfather) including the grand-dad's favorite clothes. How can dogs and cats do that? They project the image of their person to me, the dog's grandfather in that case, and I described it to the pet parent. The dog mom was astounded her dog could show me what her father used to wear almost all the time!

Like people in spirit, cats and dogs can tell me how they passed. They often make me feel their pain of passing. When I gave a talk in New York State at a fundraiser for Adirondack Save-a-Stray rescue, a woman came to me and was distressed because her dog passed. She wanted to know if her dog was okay on the other side and whether her dog had forgiven her. It was then that her little dog came through to me and made my stomach ache. He told me that he ate something out of the trash that hurt his stomach and poisoned him.

The woman was flabbergasted. She said, "How in the world did you know that's what happened?" She had come home to find the trash tipped over and rummaged through and her dog had ingested something poisonous that she had discarded. I told her that her dog showed me what he had done and that he said there was nothing to forgive. It was his own actions. He knew that his mom needed to forgive herself to heal, and he provided that message to me, to give to her.

What you should take away from these experiences is that your own cat in spirit may give you similar confirmations.

***

In part two of this book, you'll read about many different ways that cats came to their pet parents as a spirit. Pets communicate in many different ways; each based on their individual personality. To emphasize the unique nature of these different types of communication, I've organized the stories in alphabetical order by the cat's name.

###

PART 2:
Stories of Pet Spirit Communications

Chapter 7
Archie Moon Beam's Moth

Wanda, Clive, Oli and Sasha wrote me from the United Kingdom about the passing of their beautiful rescue cat named Archie Moonbeam who passed over unexpectedly only a month before.

(Photo: Archie Moonbeam. Credit: Wanda C.)

Wanda had read my Pets and the Afterlife 2 book after his passing and said, *"Your book Pets and the Afterlife 2 has given me comfort and a reason to keep believing during a time of just unreal grief."*

She went on to say that the day after he passed, a moth landed on their window with a more than uncanny resemblance to Archie. She suspected it was Archie who sent the moth with the similar pattern, and she was correct.

(Photo: Archie's Moth sign. Credit; Wanda C.)

Wanda also noted another sign from Archie came in the form of a coin. When pets want to send us a sign with a coin, they usually ask a human spirit to ensure the year on the coin is significant to them. Wanda found a coin from Archie and said,

"Also I found a 10p (pence) coin in the bathroom and I thought there is no way that this coin will be dated 2013 the year we rescued him. Lo and behold, when I looked at the date it was in fact 2013!"

When I connected with Archie, he shared a couple of personal things. I told Wanda, "He's making me feel pain in my stomach, and I'm hearing about a blood issue. It could have been feline leukemia, but it was definitely a blood issue." Wanda confirmed, "Archie died of a blood clot and had heart failure which went to his back legs leaving him unable to walk."

On additional thing Archie noted was the word, "Leo." I told Wanda that it could reference a zodiac sign (for his or your birth months), or may be something he heard, or a nickname, or related to a lion or a person's name. She confirmed that her birth zodiac sign is "Leo" and wondered if his was also Leo.

The information he shared was his way of telling his mum how closely connected they are and how much he loves her.

###

Chapter 8
Buddhi the Cat's Specific 1 Word Revelation

Whenever I do medium readings for pets, all it really takes is one personal or unique thing to identify the spirit to the person getting the reading. It can be a name, date, object, place, or anything else. In this case, a special cat named Buddhi provided a word to me that I didn't even know was a word!

I receive emails from pet parents around the world and I never know what country they are from, anything about their homes, cities, lifestyle, religious practices, or environment. That's why specific messages from pets can be so telling.

(Photo: Buddhi Credit: Ingrid)

One February, Ingrid wrote me about her cat Buddhi who passed. She said, *"I am reading your books and I am in awe over your work. We have lost our cat Buddhi unexpectedly and we are lost beyond belief. He was the center of our life and household. Just to be able to find some relief we would be so grateful if you could see anything about Buddhi. That would help us to more peace and acceptance. We are in so much pain... (as all pet lovers are of course) and what I read in your books - it does make a huge difference. Thank you from all my heart."*

When I do readings, I ask people to send a photo of their pet because there are so many pets in spirit, I need to ensure I connect with the right one. So, Ingrid sent a photo of Buddhi.

Sometimes, depending on their personalities, cats can be shy or bold in communicating. Buddhi was forthcoming about himself.

Buddhi made me feel he is quite a sharp-witted cat! I told Ingrid that he is a very intelligent, and a very, very perceptive guy who always knew what was happening. Of course, cats have an innate curiosity, but Buddhi's was deeper than that.

The next thing Buddhi told me was the kicker. I wrote Ingrid, "I keep hearing or seeing a word that starts with or sounds like "mala" - I'm unsure if that's a person, or place or thing. I can't quite tune into it." That word, a word that I was unfamiliar with, would be a key piece of information from Buddhi that immediately brought comfort as you'll read shortly in Ingrid's response.

As a medium, I often receive things that don't make any sense to me, but they do to the pet parent. This was definitely one of those times.

Buddhi went on to share with me the physical sensations that he experienced before he passed. Cats do that to help confirm their identity. I told Ingrid that Buddhi was making feel like there was a urinary issue. As I was typing the email reading at my computer, and channeling Buddhi, I kept getting that sensation. He also made me feel a tingling in my leg, which translates to a cat's right rear leg.

(Photo: Buddhi lounging on the bed Credit: Ingrid)

My reading ended with Buddhi's heartfelt love and methods that he will make direct contact with his mom.

Ingrid wrote back with a confirmation that gave me goose bumps. She said, *"Dear Rob, thank you so much for this! The word "Mala" - I shared my bedroom with Buddhi because there was friction with the other cats, so he was intimately living with me in my room. I have an altar in my bedroom and*

I use a Mala for mantra meditation. I do is early in the morning and he is always there and he hears me."

This left me stunned. Not only did I not know or understand the word, but it was intensely personal, and only Buddhi was present in Ingrid's room when she used that meditation. It's amazing what cats can convey.

Ingrid confirmed the urinary issue as well. She said, *"You are right spot on with the urinating issue. He used to urinate in all hidden corners and spots in our house and we never knew why."*

Finally, she confirmed Buddhi's presentation of his personality to me. She said, *"You are precisely right in your perception of him. That makes me so happy."*

Ingrid closed her email, *"I have a much better feeling now of him crossing over, because it is a feeling that that so cuddly, soft little love bug kept himself a contained in that frame because I needed that and he fulfilled my needs while in reality he is, as you so clearly pointed out, much deeper and more grand than I could see but my view of him is rapidly changing. I cannot thank you enough. Thank you again. I am blown away by this. God bless you."*

###

Chapter 9
Cairo Reveals His Heart Ailment

Jasmine didn't know what caused her precious cat, Cairo, to pass. She needed answers and asked me to connect with him in spirit.

Jasmine said Cairo the youngest of her two cats and he passed away one night unexpectedly. She explained that she returned home after work to feed Cairo and her other cat. She explained that he passed out after he brushed his body against her leg. For a moment, she thought he was being affectionate when he came to her instead of eating (which was usually his priority). When she reached down to pick him up to give him a kiss and he started circling around making  breathing noises. She had never seen him ever do that, and he collapsed. She realized something was terribly wrong.

Jasmine explained that she didn't know how to perform CPR on a cat and immediately called the veterinarian's office who told her to rush him there. She called a cab and on her way to the vet, she comforted Cairo in the backseat. Then she realized he had no heartbeat. She said he died so fast, and she was in shock.

Once at the veterinarian's office, she said the vet had told her what she thinks happened but couldn't be certain, and Jasmine wrote me to obtain some closure.

When Jasmine came through to me, he made me feel as if he had a heart defect. I got the sense that he found it hard to breathe, and he made me feel like a valve in the heart was malformed at birth. There was nothing that could have been done. It was not detected and couldn't be.

I told Jasmine that CPR would not have saved him and urged her not to feel guilty as there was nothing that could have been done.

Jasmine sent the following response to my reading: *"Thank you so much for responding Rob. I am in tears of relief. You know it's interesting because I called the breeder asking if the parents had a history of heart murmurs or HCM and she said she had been getting a lot of calls recently about this.*

It just startled me in another sense of relief because what the vet had told me is in his eye it looked like he suffered from a possible underlying condition. I think that litter may have had problems that's why the breeder was being flooded with phone calls of concern. Thank you so much."

###

Chapter 10
Dewey Pinpoints His Sickness and Sends Signs

As the last chapter conveyed, determining what took your precious cat's life can help bring understanding and peace. This is another reading that reflects that with a cat named Dewey who was almost 17 years old. Dewey's mom fortunately did recognize some signs he sent after his passing to confirm that he was okay in spirit.

(Photo: Dewey in a favorite spot. Credit: Jill)

Jill wrote me seeking answers to what led to Dewey's decline and ultimately his passing. A couple of months after Dewey passed she wrote me and acknowledged that she knew his time was coming but that still didn't help her prepare for his passing.

Jill said she her husband adopted Dewey when he was 8 weeks old soon after they married. Raising a cat from a baby to almost 17 is like watching a teenage human grow and the loss can be traumatic. Jill said she was having a hard time with his death and sometimes felt like she would never be over this grief or get back to her normal self again. She also acknowledged guilty feelings for not spending more time with Dewey (something that most pet parents experience).

Jill said that she and her husband knew he was suffering and was miserable and didn't want to subject him to more tests. The question of the cause of his decline was unanswered and troubling.

Dewey Sent Signs
Jill noted that she read one of my Pets and the Afterlife books and picked up on some of the signs that Dewey sent after his passing. The included a musical sign, a dream and influencing and insect and a bird.

Dewey's Musical Sign
Jill said, *"The day I went to the vet to pick up his ashes they were playing a song on the radio that has been a song that has always touched me. It is Dolly Parton's song "I Will Always Love You" but Whitney Houston was singing it. I immediately thought it was odd hearing that song as I haven't heard it in forever and couldn't believe I was hearing it at that exact moment. I knew it had to be a message from Dewey."*

That song by Dolly Parton happens to be one of my favorites, too, and because it's about someone who will always love someone but must move on, it's a perfect sign from spirit.

60

Dewey's Dreams and Influences

Jill noted that a month after Dewey's passing, she had a visitation dream. Those kinds of dreams are deeper and more real feeling. Often during those dreams, you can feel a pet's fur, or smell their scent.

Jill said, *"It was completely different from a regular dream. It seemed so real, like I wasn't even sleeping, and he came and curled up next to my head on my pillow. It was so comforting and so vivid! I will always treasure that gift from Dewey."*

She also noticed the odd behavior of a ladybug and cardinal. Spirits can influence birds and insects to behave oddly whenever we're thinking of the spirit, so we will understand they are around.

My Reading with Dewey

Pets in spirit do not want us to feel guilty for not spending more time with them. They understand we must "do things," and they are often content just to be in the same room. That's what unconditional love is to them – so long as they're loved they are content.

Dewey answered the question of his passing by sharing his pain of passing by making me feel a pain in my kidneys. I took that to indicate renal failure. I explained that if Dewey was drinking a lot before he passed, that would be an indication. He also made my throat feel dry and made me feel as if I were thirsty.

Jill's Response

Jill responded to the reading and said that she thought she could now find some closure. She wrote, *"I wasn't sure what Dewey had died from, but I initially thought cancer. When you mentioned renal failure, I looked up the symptoms and couldn't believe it. They matched the same symptoms Dewey had and the cancer symptoms.*

What caught my eyes though were that with renal failure, seizures are one of the symptoms and Dewey was having seizures and my husband and I didn't know what was causing them.

Dewey had a large growth on his right side that grew quite rapidly and was in the same area as his kidney. He was also very dehydrated the vet had told us and was probably why he was so thirsty. He was drinking a lot of water all the time but had no appetite.

I think you are right and that is why he died. I feel happy knowing he was ready to go and is not upset with me for having him put to sleep.

God bless you and thanks again for taking the time to write me, a complete stranger, and offering me some comfort at this very difficult time."

Pets can provide us with answers from the other side, and sometimes when we get these messages, we must try and make sense of them, as Jill and her husband did by matching what Dewey told me with the symptoms of renal failure.

It's also comforting to know that he was so persistent about sending signs to his pet parents, and that they were able to recognize them.

###

Chapter 11
Draik on the Move and His Yellow Mouse

Cats are extremely perceptive. They understand when they go from one place to another, and like people, they have great memories and they hold those memories dear, just like a favorite object. In this chapter, you'll meet a childhood cat named Draik who came through to provide messages of comfort to Vann.

(Photo: Draik relaxing at home. Credit: Vann)

On October 26, 2021, Vann had listened to the Unsolved Mysteries podcast episode about my abilities and readings. Vann said, *"It really struck a chord with me, having lost my childhood pet this last year. And I was hoping that I could get a reading scheduled, no matter how long it takes. My pet's name is Draik, and he passed back on April 7. I just want to know that he was happy. And whether he feels I let him down in the end. He meant the word world to me. Thank you so much."*

Whenever I communicate with a cat or dog in spirit, their messages can be similar in terms of love, but there's always one or more unique things that stand out and really resonate with the pet parent.

Draik came through to me as being very content in spirit.

On the Move
The first thing he told me was that Vann moved but it didn't matter where they lived. I told Vann: Draik said it didn't matter where you lived, because whenever you were around, he always felt the love was always there.   Did he ever go with you somewhere? It feels like he either moved with you for a time or went on a ride with you somewhere. Regardless, it didn't matter because it was always " home" being near you.

Vann Confirms
Vann confirmed the sense of moving. Vann said, *"Thank you so much, Rob! This truly did bring me some peace regarding my baby. I'd like to share with you some details that really struck home with me.*

I did move with him multiple times. I even brought him with me when I ran hours away from home as a teenager. I was only gone for about a month before coming all the way back home with him again. He's taken a few long car rides due to that, and later with visiting my parents who do in fact live a long seven hours drive away."

Draik Conveys Passing

The second thing that Vann was struck by was Draik's messages of passing. The reading continued: He's making me feel like his kidneys were a cause of his passing. I'm feeling issues in my kidneys right now. He's giving me the sense that you may not have been around the day he passed, but that doesn't matter.

Vann said, *"As for his passing, he absolutely was having kidney failure, along with other troubles. We drove him to the vet before they even opened to be there as soon as they would let us in, and we could let them know that it was an emergency. They gave him an x-ray and I'm not sure what other tests as I was distraught. I honestly can't remember those details. However, the consensus was that his organs, kidneys especially, were either in the process of, or already had shut down. Our only choice was euthanasia. It was not much of a choice, though it was the hardest one I've ever had to make. But I knew there was nothing more we could do for him, and he was suffering greatly. I was there with him, but he'd seemed to have left consciousness behind the night before his appointment, when he took a turn for the worst, and that may well have occurred before I arrived back home from work.*

Draik's Toy Request

Our pets do not want us to dwell on their passing and want their parents to remember good memories.

I wrote Vann: Draik shared with me a memory of being in your bedroom when you were younger. Sitting on the bed watching you - perhaps at a desk with a light on, either studying or reading something. He was just content to be in the same room. Now, in spirit, he visits you from time to time.

He's showing me a toy he had, actually several - one was a small blue stuffed toy, the other yellow, and both looked like little mice. Do you have one of those? He would be honored if you put one of his toys (or even his collar) on your desk. He is showing me a desk, near his picture.

Draik's Toy Has a New Desk

Vann wrote me about Draik's toy message: *"We did once have a toy mouse with a yellow tail made with feathers that he was fond of. He was a very lazy and laid-back boy, so he didn't play often, though he did like that one. If you teased him with a toy, he would typically ignore it or just watch rather than play, but occasionally he would swipe out at it just once like he simply couldn't control the urge any longer! Then would act as if he embarrassed himself. He would do that with that mouse.*

I think that specific toy might have been thrown and replaced possibly even before he passed but it's possible it's hiding under the couch or somewhere else so I will be looking out for it in case he's suggesting that he's still finding it when he visits.

I did take one of the current mouse toys in the house and immediately put it up on the desk as a placeholder in the meantime. I'm attaching a photo of the desk where his pictures have hung over since only a couple of days after his passing.

You've given me such a blessing that I'm overwhelmed. Thank you so much for what you do for all of us broken pet lovers and bringing us peace. You yourself are an angel. Thank you."

The original toy has since been found and placed in its new and proper home.

A Comforting Note from Vann

I asked Vann if there was a sense of comfort after the connection and received this wonderful note that I will always treasure.

Vann wrote: "*Rob mentioned to me a desire that Draik wanted his toy mouse to sit on my desk with his photos. I hung this collage of him above my desk two days after his passing to keep his memory strong.*

Rob picked up this information with nothing more than a name and photo of my boy. That is how I knew that he really was here after he passed away. To have known those were there in any capacity was astounding. I immediately put a toy mouse up on the desk to keep Draik occupied, and I've felt lighter since that moment. I haven't felt this much peace since he left me that day. Eternally grateful for Rob and his willingness to share his abilities for the sake of animal lovers everywhere."

###

Chapter 12
Fritzie's "1113" and Bird Signs

On April, Mike wrote me about the recent passing of his cat, Fritzie. Mike was dealing with anxiety over her being beyond his reach and frightened or in need of help. Like many pet parents who have lost a precious cat, he said he's been somewhat paralyzed with fear over losing her. He said, *"She has never been out of my care, and I'd always had anxiety over keeping her safe...you can well imagine the trauma I suffered when I lost her on January 6 of this year."*

(Photo: Fritze hiding in a laundry basket. Credit: Mike)

When I connected with Fritzie she told me a number of things, but several really stood out to Mike. I told him that "One sign is a small bird that has been lingering around your house in the last week and singing. The bird is being influenced by Fritzie to get his attention."

Then Fritzie was specific about a number she gave me. I told Mike, "She's showing me "1113" - That could be a time, or a month and day. - and any of those numbers may be significant to her (or you)." The number was a puzzle for Mike to solve, and he did.

First, Mike responded about Fritzie's message about the signing bird close to his house. Mike said, *"Yes, there is a bird nested with her babies right on my bedroom windowsill!"* That means that Fritzie influenced that bird to build her nest right next to Mikes' window, so that he would know she's close by.

I provided other signs to Mike, which he took comfort from. He was puzzled by the number message, though, but it would become clear. He wrote, *"I'll never let her go in my heart and even as I'm crying tears as I write this, one day I'll see her in Heaven....I certainly will try to find the meaning of 1113."*

A couple of days later, Mike messaged me on social media about the 1113 message. He said, *"Mr. Gutro....I looked through my photos on my iPad which have many different kinds of subjects in it....and looked up which photos I have dated 1113, or this past November 13 ... and there is only one picture on that date..."*

The photo Mike sent dated November 13, 2017 and it was especially meaningful, since it was a photo of Fritzie and it had a special meaning. It was a picture of Fritzie hiding behind the large leaves of a plant.

Initially, Mike didn't know what to make of that photo. When I saw it, Fritzie's message was clear. I told Mike that the photo of her hiding behind the plant means that she's watching him from spirit even though he may not be able to see her. It's almost as if she's hiding behind a large plant and he can't see her. That's just how it is from spirit. Spirits are around us and we can't necessarily see them!

(Photo: November 13, 2017, this was the only photo Mike took that day was a very symbolic photo. And it was especially meaningful. It was a picture of Fritzie hiding behind the large leaves of a plant. Credit: Mike)

Mike responded, *"That is EXACTLY what I thought when I saw that picture...Even though she may be hidden, she's with me and watching me....I was so happy to see that picture on 11/13.*

Thank you so much Mr. Gutro...your reading is a Godsend...and spot on. I'm so grateful. God bless you."

###

Chapter 13
Fudge and the Tropical Plants

I never know what personal sign a spirit is going to give me. One cat was adamant about showing me tropical plants for a reason only his mother would know.

When I received Karen's email, she only noted that he was a cat who passed. Here is the email she wrote, *"Hello Rob, I found your blog and your page and am emailing you to ask for your kind assistance. Please.*

I know that you are extremely busy, and your time is very precious, and ask that some day when you see this, you would consider communicating with my beautiful boy Fudge, who passed on 5 October 2017. I'm absolutely devastated and struggling to cope with his tragic and sudden passing. I desperately need to hear from him I miss him so much. I just want him back irrational as that is. If you can find it in your heart to help me, I will be eternally grateful.

Thank you and regards, Karen"

Fudge's Messages

I was able to connect with Fudge and I provided Karen with a number of signs to look for from Fudge. However, one thing that Fudge showed me struck me as odd. Especially because it was in winter that I did the reading, although I realize whatever season it is has no influence on a message from spirit. I wrote to Karen, "He's showing me a warm place with tropical-like plants and says he was there. - I'm unsure if you went on a vacation or into a greenhouse (he doesn't know either, because he's only sharing the image with me).

However, even Lowes and Home Depot have greenhouses with tropical plants."

(Photo: Fudge poses. Credit: Karen)

I wrote the "Lowes" and "Home Depot" because I assumed Karen was located in the U.S.A., where I live. I learned in a later email she sent that she's actually from South Africa! That's why mediums should just pass along what they see from spirit, and not try to interpret the signs (or give local store names, for that matter).

Regardless, Karen fully understood the message and knew it was indeed Fudge. She said, *"He used to travel with me in my car as a little boy to visit my family, they have an atrium full of huge plants and greenery, it's very warm there. I visit regularly.*

Fudge loved car travel. I'm really happy that he's visiting, I miss him terribly and I will try to be calmer though it's hard most days."

I was amazed how Fudge shared the image of the tropical plants and the atrium and indicated that it was special. This is a great example of how a pet's spirit can provide a unique sign relevant to their lives, to help identify that they are around.

###

Chapter 14
Geoffrey Conveys His Passing

Geoffrey was born on May 16, 2002, and passed away on August 10, 2020. Jennifer contacted me after Geoffrey's passing to get some closure. During his reading he conveyed his memories and feelings of his life and passing. This chapter also contains a special "biography," something you could write about your cat to bring healing.

(Photo: Geoffrey posing. Credit: Jennifer)

When I looked at Geoffrey's photo, he made me feel a big empty feeling in my stomach, especially on the left side. It felt like cancer and it was eating at him from the inside. I physically felt that sensation while doing the reading.

He also made me feel exhausted. He showed me his droopy eyelids. I also felt like he was falling asleep sitting up.

He continued sharing his physical sensations and I felt totally worn out. Then I experienced a sudden jabbing pain in my right hip. He said it was injection, and it made my right leg tingle. He conveyed it didn't hurt, and he began feeling sleepy and became more peaceful. Then I felt his last breath. It felt like a big sigh of relief. He had shared the physical feelings of his last moments.

Until now, no pet spirit I've connected with shared the physical sensations they experienced while being put to sleep.

Donna, Jennifer's mother, wrote me after the reading and noted, *"Jennifer said that you described his last few days exactly. He was falling asleep sitting up and was so weak at times he couldn't stand up using his hind legs."*

As a side note, Donna noted Geoffrey had 6 toes on all of his feet. I told her because the number 6 unique to Geoffrey, it will also be a call sign from him.

***

My Recommendation: Write Your Pet's Biography
To help through the grieving process, I recommend writing down some special memories of your cat to help remember and celebrate your pet's life. It could be about your cat's adoption, a special day in your cat's life, their personality, or any other event. Jennifer did that and asked to share some things about Geoffrey's life because he was so special.

Jennifer's Bio of Geoffrey

Jennifer said, *"I adopted Geoffrey on July 13, 2002, through a co-worker who knew of someone whose cat had just had a litter of six kittens. At the time, I was only 24, living by myself and working my first real full-time job. I decided that I wanted a companion and despite never having had a kitten before and not knowing the first thing about them. The instant I saw Geoffrey, I knew he was the one. At only 1.6 pounds, he was all ears and feet, a polydactyl black and tan tabby with a racing stripe down his back and what looked like actual thumbs. As it was just the two of us, Geoffrey and I bonded instantly. He was adventurous and full of personality. He used his big feet to swat flies out of mid-air. When we picked him up, he would flip light switches and perform tight-wire acts across the top of my sliding glass door blinds, which he accessed via top of the refrigerator.*

When my husband moved in, they became fast friends. In 2004, we adopted Madison, a solid gray kitten, who proved to be the complete opposite of Geoffrey. At first, he did not care for the new member of the family, but he slowly learned to tolerate her. He loved using his big paw to pop her in the head from time to time when she got too close or just looked at him the wrong way.

After our two boys were born, Geoffrey started to settle down. He still would cop an attitude with us, would growl when trying to clip the nails on his extra toes and spent many a morning "singing" and howling, waking us up way too early for work and school. But he loved to lie in the sunshine, head butt us every chance he had and take naps with us on the couch. He loved greeting the boys when they came home from school every day and sat there patiently on the floor while they both got down for "The Pet Crew," petting and rubbing his cheeks.

At the end of July 2020, Geoffrey's behavior started to change. He started sleeping much more, falling into such a deep sleep that he would fall off the couch or face first into pillows. At the beginning of August, his appetite severely decreased, he started losing even more weight from his already thin frame and occasionally had trouble with his back legs. A weekend visit to the vet offered some brief hope, but it was not meant to be. Upon returning from his appointment, he ceased eating completely, his breathing became fast and labored at times and his energy was gone. We knew the time was coming. On Monday, August 10, 2020, I had to make probably one of the toughest decisions of my life. At 3 p.m., he passed away with assistance, with me and my son by his side.

Geoffrey had been with me through every stage thus far in my adult life. From living on my own, to getting married, to purchasing my first house, two children and every full-time job I have ever had. For 18 years, he was the constant in my life. Although he has now passed on, I am comforted in knowing that our decision was the right one and that he was thankful and appreciative for the life he had and for helping him when he needed it the most."

***

By writing down your cat's story, you will forever preserve memories of them that may otherwise fade over time. It also helps you realize how your cat was with you through good and bad times and taught you the meaning of unconditional love. That love will forever bind you together.

###

Chapter 15
Ghostly Cat I Met in Ellicott City

It's rare that a pet will opt to stay as an earthbound ghost and not cross over. When cats and other animals pass away, they see the light to the other side and sense there is nothing but love and peace there, so it's almost an immediate draw. There are few exceptions, however. Very few cats decide to stay behind on earth as a ghost, but only if there's something they can't let go. That's exactly what happened with the cat I encountered in a salon in Ellicott City, Maryland.

(Image: Rob's sketch of the shadow of the ghostly cat that still lives in the Envy Salon as he saw the cat briefly on the second floor. Credit: Rob Gutro)

In 2017, I was asked to interview with Television Producer Tony Hoos of the Howard County Community College. He interviewed me for a video segment about how pets communicate from the afterlife. The video featured businesses in the county and the Envy Salon was the topic of this shoot. The video in the series "A Few Odd Minutes (in Howard County)" can be found here on the Community College's website: https://youtu.be/a7-0IUOqoFw.

(Photo: Rob saw the ghost cat scamper from the dresser into the room on the right side. Credit: R. Gutro)

The Envy Salon is known to be haunted by a cat who has been seen by employees and patrons of the shop. Leeza Ennis, a hairstylist and manager of Envy was also interviewed. She explained that the land where the salon's two-story brick building sits was purchased in 1842 from the Ellicott Brothers from Pennsylvania, who moved to Maryland founded mills and the town of what is now known as "Old Ellicott City."

In the video, Leeza explained that there are two benign ghosts who live in the salon. One is a woman, the other a cat. She explained employees used to do nails on the first floor in a room located off the reception area. One day, a nail tech had a child with him that was about 3 years old. The child turned toward the stairs and said, "kitty." There was no living cat in the building. Children often see ghosts or spirits because they are open-minded.

Leeza explained that in the main styling area when she was working on a client, both she and the client looked under the chair because they heard a cat! Again, there was no living cat in the building. Later in the 2 minute 14 second video, Leeza explained her experience with the human ghost of the woman named Catherine.

During my visit there, I did encounter the ghost cat, but Catherine chose to remain quiet. When I entered the salon's front door into first level, I sensed a human ghost but couldn't get an idea of who she was. I later learned about Catherine and that she is usually active after business hours. Catherine is thought to be a former resident when it was a home.

Once I understood that the human ghost didn't want to communicate, I walked up the stairs to the second floor. As I did, I developed a headache which indicates I'm in the presence of an earthbound ghost. When I reached the top of the stairs, I saw a small hallway that connected rooms with other hair and nail stations. There was a dresser there with a rectangular carpet in front of it. On that carpet, in front of the dresser sat a ghost cat in shadow, who quickly ran into a room off the hallway.

Ghosts, like spirits who cross over, appear as dark shadows when they don't have enough energy to become fully visible in color. You may see you cat in spirit as a dark shadow. It doesn't mean they're earthbound. It just means when they visit from spirit, they don't have enough energy to become visible.

As I walked around the second floor, I caught a second glimpse of a small, dark shadow zipping out of the room where ghost cat previously entered. The shadow then bolted down the stairway to the first floor, just like a scared cat would.

Earthbound ghosts and spirits can sense which living people can see them. The ghost cat knew I could see him, so he ran.

However, your cat behaved in the physical they will behave the same way in the afterlife. If your cat was skittish and ran from people they didn't know, they would also do that from the other side. If they welcomed strangers, then in spirit, they would linger.

I never learned this cat's name because he didn't want to "talk" with me.

(Photo: The stairway the ghost cat ran down. Credit: R. Gutro)

Over years of paranormal investigations, I have only encountered one other ghost cat. That cat was in a home and didn't belong to the family that was currently living there. The story is featured in chapter 16 of my book Lessons Learned from Talking to the Dead.

It's very rare for a cat to decide to stay as an earthbound ghost. Most pets cross over into the light and wait for us on the other side. This particular cat in the Envy Salon had his reasons for staying, he just didn't want to talk about them.

###

Chapter 16
Gracie's Answer was Blowing in the Wind

There are many ways that our pets communicate from spirit. In August 2017, a very special cat named Gracie came to me in spirit and indicated she would use something in nature to let her mom know she's still around. Gracie's unique sign would be "blowing in the wind."

(Photo: Gracie at the window. Credit: Linda)

Linda wrote: *"I lost my cat, Gracie, to kidney disease. She was 15. As you know the pain is deep and (emotionally) paralyzing. She hasn't communicated with me yet and I'm panicky about that. So, I'm writing to you in hopes that it will stimulate her to contact me through you."*

When I connected with Gracie, she shared with me some of the physical feelings that she experienced before she passed. After I conveyed those to her mom, Linda recognized them from medical conditions that Gracie had before she passed.

After the physical sensations, Gracie changed topics. She confirmed that she was trying to communicate with Linda but noticed that Linda wasn't picking up her signs. Then Gracie told me she recently used a leaf blowing near Linda's face/head as a means of conveying her playful presence. Gracie also wanted her mom to watch for the signs of leaves. I asked Linda if she recalled a leaf blowing near her head/face recently, and she responded, "No." That just meant that Gracie was going to do it sometime soon.

Less than a month later, Gracie made that sign happen. On Sept 7, Linda sent me a photo and wrote me the following email, proving that Gracie was still with her. Linda's email said, "I had to write you!! In early August, I emailed you about my cat, Gracie, who I had put to sleep the end of July because of kidney failure. I was upset because I hadn't received any signs from her letting me know she's okay."

"At that time, you told me that she had been trying to let me know she's okay and I couldn't pick up on it because of my grief. You said she had been using a leaf, blowing near my face/head. Well, I wasn't going to be able to believe that because I live in the Midwest and this time of year there are leaves falling/blowing everywhere, all the time. Since then, I have been asking her every night to please send me a sign, so I'll know that she's somewhere and still loves me.

I have a managed colony of feral cats and I washed the feral cats' bowls today and dried them with some white terrycloth towels (which I have never EVER used before, I've ALWAYS used paper towels and immediately throw them away). I then tossed the towels on the garage step (paper towels wouldn't have been there). The towels never touched the ground. I didn't walk on the towels. I had nothing on my hands. I closed the overhead garage door (no wind blowing in).

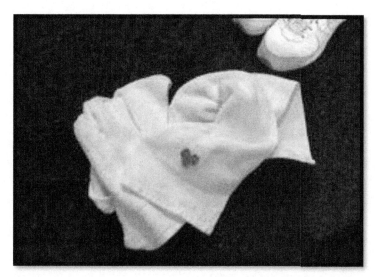

(Photo: A heart-shaped leaf "mysteriously" appeared on Linda's towel. Credit: Linda)

Two hours later I opened the door to the garage and saw this… A HEART shaped LEAF!!!! Right in my path!!!"

Spirits always find a way to let us know they're around. It was also obvious that Gracie (with human help in spirit) nudged Linda to contact me in August, so she would be aware of the sign that Gracie left in September. There are no such things as coincidences. If you get a reading from a medium about something your pet conveyed, you may not understand it or see it immediately, but always keep it in mind. It takes a lot of planning, energy, and effort for spirits to make their messages come through to us. Always be on watch!

###

Chapter 17
Harvey: A Lesson in Overcoming Guilt

Jennie wrote me and conveyed feelings of guilt regarding her late cat, whom I'll call Harvey. It's normal for pet parents to experience guilt for one reason or another. Some agonize over having made the decision too early or too late to help their cat cross. Others feel guilt for not spending enough time together.

Jennie noted that in September of 2020, Harvey became very ill. Her veterinarian told her Harvey was severely anemic and that a blood transfusion would only prolong his life by a few days before he would need another one. She had to make the choice and had him euthanized because she didn't want him to suffer. She wrote, *"I'm heartbroken and feeling tremendous guilt."*

Her guilt stemmed from making the decision to help Harvey pass to sometimes shouting at him for his actions. Jennie wrote, *"For over a year I had spent very little time petting him or allowing him to snuggle with me. I was very stressed out and short tempered. I never hit him but raised my voice, sometimes yelled when he would come behind me and bang his head against the back of my knee while I was trying to fix his meals.*

But I'm so angry at myself for treating him the way I did. I wish he knew how much I love him and that he was my little angel."

I explained that whether you are a pet parent or human parent, it's normal to sometimes be agitated or irritated at behavior of your "kids." Because our pets can read our emotional energy, they understand when we're under stress and know why we react badly. That's why sometimes if they know they've done something wrong, when you're happy, sad, stressed, peaceful, lonely and need affection, irritated and need space, happy or sad.

Jennie understood that Harvey could hear her from spirit, and she would continue to talk with him. She mentioned she received his ashes and was keeping them close to her.

When pets are living with us, they can read our emotional energy, and understand when we agonize over the decision to help them pass. But they always appreciate us finding the courage to do what's right for them. These are all important things to know because they don't want us to feel badly or carry feelings of guilt. They know it takes a lot of courage, and it is the ultimate lesson of the unconditional love they try to teach us.

###

Chapter 18
Jillian's Spirit Has Another Cat Mimic Habits

When our pets pass, they can influence living animals to mimic their behaviors and habits to convey their presence to us. In this case, a cat named Jillian did exactly that with a neighborhood cat. Jillian's mom, Carolyn, was familiar with a neighborhood cat who had never before paid a visit to her home until after Jillian passed. This neighborhood cat appeared to sit in Jillian's spot outside and roll over as Jillian did when seeking attention.

In November 2021, Carolyn wrote me about sings she knew were from Jillian. She said, *"I believe Jillian, my cat that was tragically killed by a predator, has been communicating very strongly finally—or I am finally open to receiving as the extreme grief passes some."*

(Photo: Coco in her special spot. Credit: Carolyn R.)

"There is a calico cat named, Coco, who lives 5 doors up and she has never come to visit, but I would see her on my walks as she is very friendly."

*(Photo: Jillian in her usual spot, that Coco now takes.
Credit: Carolyn R.)*

"One day recently, Coco was on my front porch, and I went out and sat down and loved on her. She flipped and flopped on the pavement as Jillian used to do with me. After about 10 minutes, I needed to go inside to get on with my day and I walked into my home office.

There is a French door to the back patio and Jillian would sit right by the door and look in when she wanted my attention or a snack. I began working in the office and turned around to get something and there was Coco, sitting in this same spot exactly as Jillian would have done.

I went out on the back patio as I could not resist. She began loving on me and flipping and flopping on the concrete again just like Jillian. I knew for sure Jillian was with us and had brought Coco to do exactly as she has done for years, as you indicated in your books. I spoke to Jillian and thanked her so much for loving me through Coco that day and told her how much I missed her.

Coco has come back to visit a few more times, but not to the back patio, to that spot, until just recently.

Now I know Jillian is sending Coco (the neighbor's cat) to me when she appears in Jillian's spot. I am so grateful to have this spiritual connection."

###

Chapter 19
Leo's Abundance of Different Signs

Lisa lost her beloved cat Leo on November 13, 2020. Leo was 10 years old, a black Norwegian Forest tuxedo cat weighing about 17 pounds and he was very smart. In fact, he proved his intelligence with a bounty of different signs from spirit. Leo became very active in his communications from the other side, to ensure his mom would not get lost in her grief. She conveyed signs to me, and Leo provided me with some explanations. In this chapter, you'll read about the many ways that Leo communicated from dreams to look-alikes and more.

(Image: One of Lisa's favorite photos of Leo. Sadly, this was the exact same spot Lisa found him just before he passed. Credit: Lisa N.)

Lisa is a dedicated cat mom, and she's also sensitive to spirit. She recounted that she had visitation dreams of her father and other pets. She's found signs ranging from finding whiskers and hearing purrs from cats who have passed, in addition to spirit appearances. She recalled that she visibly saw her cat Cuba's tail wrap around her bed post and go under her bed 2 weeks after Cuba's passing! She also saw her father's spirit in the corner of a room.

Leo passed before Lisa came home from work. Our pets can choose to pass alone or with loved ones around. When pets choose the former, it's because they know it would likely be too traumatic for us to see them pass and they don't want their passing to be the last memory we have of them.

Lisa's connection to Leo gave her a sense of his passing that occurred while she was at work. She said, *"I had wanted to come home at lunch time that day and didn't, so put off my weird feelings. I felt massive guilt that I could have saved Leo had I come home earlier."*

Later that day as she was driving home from work, she felt an urgency to get home as fast as she could. She said it was so strong she started cursing at a red light. She didn't know where her energy and sense of urgency was coming from to hurry home and then she arrived to find Leo had passed.

When I began communicating with Leo, Lisa's dad stepped forward first. The sense of urgency Lisa felt waiting at the red light was her dad's spirit trying to nudge her home so she could be there with Leo as soon as possible.

After Lisa's dad stepped back, Leo conveyed the reason for his passing. He made me feel a pain in the heart area. That indicated that there was a heart issue that led to his passing.

He indicated that there was nothing that could have been done to prolong his life as it was a congenital issue from birth.

Lots of Dreams
Lisa noted that after Leo passed, he was quite active. He came to her in dreams for a couple of months. The night of his passing, as she was drifting to sleep, she saw him on the floor below her bed for about 3 seconds. She said Leo was belly up, in his comfort position. I told Lisa that he did that because he knew she understood it was his comfort position and it was a way to convey he is now okay in spirit.

In another dream, she saw Leo morphing from a pure black cat into a black and white cat, which was what he was. I explained to Lisa that the metamorphosis dream was his way of letting her know that he transitioned into spirit on the other side.

Later, Lisa had a spirit visit. That's deeper than a dream and sometimes includes a tactile experience. Lisa said, *"I had a dream about him at 4 o'clock this morning. First time in a long while, I got to hold and pet him, smell him and kiss him."*

Whiskers
Another sign that Leo provided was two whiskers Lisa found after his passing. I explained that even though Lisa may have been looking for them, Leo put them where she could find them to let her know he is visiting.

Doppelgangers
Lisa said she saw an exact look-alike of Leo on one of her walking routes to work one day. She said, *"I almost fell over! I thought it was him! It spooked me so much I even called his name Leo out loud and chased the cat around the corner."*

A Painted Stone, Feathers, and a Favorite Scent

Lisa always kept an eye out for signs from Leo. While walking in her neighborhood, she found a beautiful small painted stone with the word love and 3 red flowers on it. She had a realization the letters in Leo's name make up 75% of the word "Love."

Leo was also dropping lots of black and white feathers in Lisa's path as well. Spirits will manipulate feathers to let us know they are around. They can also use favorite scents - like perfumes, cigars, or food. In Leo's case, it was bacon! Lisa noted that the weekend Leo passed, she smelled the scent of bacon coming from someone else's house. Bacon was Leo's favorite treat on weekends.

His Nickname in the Physical

Spirits can lead us to things that remind us of them. Lisa called him "panda bear" because of his tuxedo appearance. Within seven weeks of his passing, Lisa noted she had "seen plenty of images of panda bears." That's not a coincidence.

Other Cats Seeing Leo in Spirit

Lisa's other cats also recognized Leo's spirit visit. She said that her cat Lucy sometimes stares intently where Leo used to sleep in bed. Pets in spirit will do the same things they did when they were in the physical. So, it makes sense that Leo would come back for a visit in spirit and sit in the bed he used to sleep in. Because living pets have a different physiology in their eyes and can see faster movement, they can see spirits when they visit, because they move at a higher vibration.

***

Leo provided examples of a lot of different methods that our pets in spirit communicate with us. We can all learn a lot from Leo!

###

Chapter 20
Levin's Passing, Detailed Visitation, Sounds

There are several parts to this chapter about a special cat named Levin. In the first part, Levin chose the time and place of his passing, as some of our pets (and humans) do for reasons of their own. The second part is an amazing and detailed vision that came to Levin's pet mom when she was in a state of deep relaxation.

When we find ourselves in a relaxed state, we are more open to visitations from spirit. Levin also gave signs through noises from actions that he did when he was in the physical, as our pets tend to do from spirit.

(Image: Levin poses. Credit: Rhonda)

Levin Chooses His Passing

Rhonda wrote me about her terminally ill kitty named Levin who had passed the previous week. After he passed, she began reading my Pets and the Afterlife 2 book. She wrote, *"I fear I made a horrible mistake!"*

She explained Levin was diagnosed with a cancerous tumor in his chest in November 2018 and she and her family were told there was no hope for recovery, so they began hospice care. The tumor obstructed his esophagus and caused a build-up of fluid in his chest that severely diminished his ability to breathe. They used medications to temporarily ease the symptoms. He hated taking the medication and she hated forcing it on him.

Rhonda explained Levin was restless on January 16, 2019, the day before he passed. Several times that day he went out to sit under his favorite tree. That night, she knew the end was near, so every time he moved to a different room, Rhonda followed. The next day, she noted Levin was clearly in distress, with open mouth breathing. She let him out to sit under his tree one last time in the snow, then put him up in a window so he could see the squirrels one last time.

Rhonda explained, *"Here's where I fear I made a terrible mistake; I promised him that he would never have to go back to the vet's office again. He was terrified of it. I promised him that he could die at home surrounded by his other pet family and us, his parents. His struggle to get his breath was more than difficult to watch. The pitiful look in his eyes broke my heart. Finally, we found him hiding under the bed and I made the decision to help end his terrible suffering.*

When we got into the car, he began to struggle. I knew that he knew where we were going. During the short drive he pulled free from me. He threw his head back on the console, gasped for air and was gone. I feel like I betrayed him, Rob. I promised I wouldn't make him go back there and he became so stressed that he died in the car. I feel horrible. I think he wanted to die alone under the bed in his own home where the sights and sounds were familiar and comforting. I don't know if I can forgive myself."

Why Levin Choose to Pass in the Car
I explained to Rhonda that Levin said he passed in the car because he didn't want to go to the vet. It wasn't fear of the vet that took him. He was meant to pass then and if Rhonda had not taken him in the car he would have passed at the same exact time at home.

Levin passed as he wanted, with Rhonda. I explained there was nothing to feel guilty about as Rhonda did what any concerned pet parent would do, and Levin understood that. Pets, like people either want to be with their loved ones when they pass or be by themselves. Levin appreciated being surrounded by family, even if it was in the car.

Levin's Window Sign
Two days after Levin's death, Rhonda and her husband Dana were watching TV when they both heard the noise that Levin used to make on their back door when he wanted to come inside. Rhonda said, *"Levin always got up and 'window washed.' We could hear his paws squeaking on the window. Dana got up to go see who was at the door, and we were both surprised to see that no one was there."* Because pets do the same things in spirit as they did in life, Levin continued to paw the window as a spirit to let his parents know he's okay and still around.

Levin Brings Many Other Spirit Pets in a Spirit Visit
Three days after Levin's passing, Rhonda experienced a very real visit from Levin, and it seems that a special song acted

as the impetus. Her entire vision lasted for the length of the song, and many of her pets appeared. She saw her previous cats, dogs and iguanas all come in. Rhonda explained it seemed so real, almost like she had no control over how it played out. Following is Rhonda's experience and unless otherwise noted, most pets named are cats:

*"I was soaking in the bathtub listening to a music playlist on my phone from Final Fantasy VIII. Levin and I listened to it frequently when we napped. I had picked a song from it before he passed and **told him it was our song.** It's called Melodies of Life. As I was soaking in the tub, I was leaning against the wall with my eyes closed crying because I missed Levin so much. I told him that I knew my grief would hinder my ability to receive any communication from him, but all I really wanted to know was that he was alright. I wanted to know that he was happy and reunited with my other fur babies.*

As I lay there with my eyes still closed, the tears stopped and as our song began to play on my phone, I saw Levin in a circle of light. At first it was just his face surrounded by the light. He drew closer and then I realized I was standing outside by a tree in the back yard that we call the cat tree.

Years ago, we placed boards and perches at varying levels for the cats to play on because the yard was fenced in. Levin was in the tree and filled my entire field of vision as he got closer and closer. I reached out and hugged him. He seemed so large! But I put my arms around his neck and cried happy tears to see him once more. As he stepped back from me, one by one, my other fur angels began appearing. [My spirit cats] Puffles and Spencer right behind him. Right behind Levin was a little kitten we'd lost years ago, Gracie. She was still a kitten. I picked her up and cuddled her. She was so soft and fluffy. On the left side of the tree was Twelve, heavier than I'd ever seen him. Boo Boo came down from the top left of the tree larger than life. Spencer was young again as was Puffles. I saw Shasta on the very far left branch also young and healthy. I looked down at the ground and saw Shiloh my Jack Russell/Beagle mix who passed in 2007 playing with Kira our Husky who had just passed a year ago. Both looked as they had at their healthiest.

I picked Shiloh up and hugged him playing with his cute beagle ears. I recalled that he had passed during the night while I was asleep. Twice during the vision, I started to apologize to two of the dogs for them having died without me being present, but I heard a voice say, 'There are no sad thoughts here.'

I patted Kira on the head and the two continued to play. I looked up in the tree beside Shasta and my iguana Samson was coming down a branch toward me. I reached over and stroked her head. My other iguanas Toby and Gidget were near her. Up in the tree to my right I saw Chi Chi. I never got to touch her but then my attention was drawn out through the yard toward the bird house where I saw my white German Shepherd, Keisha running toward me with a little black puppy I'd named Bear. I remembered that Bear died of Parvovirus without me being in the room with him. I began to tell him how sorry I was that he had died alone, but again a voice interrupted me saying 'There are no negative thoughts here.' The same phrase both times.

I saw one of my babies that I never expected to see. My possum Pierre from my childhood coming down a branch on the right side near my head. They were all there! Together.

As the song was coming to an end on my phone, Levin stepped to the front and filled my field of vision again. He was glowing and beautiful. Slowly, he and the circle of light began growing smaller and finally faded away. I opened my eyes, and it was all gone. The song had ended, and I was still soaking. I waited as the next song came on hoping to recreate the vision, but in my heart, I knew that was all I was going to get, because really that's all I'd asked for. Just to know he was healthy and with his friends again. The experience left me smiling instead of sad to see them go. It was a healing experience.

I'm still missing Levin and the others and I'll still cry, but for a moment, there was an unbelievable peace and joy that I hope I never forget."

***

Do All Past Pets Usually Come into a Visit?
Rhonda's vision of Levin and many of her other pets in spirit was both amazing and rare. Although our pets are all together on the other side, usually the one who passed most recently is the one who will provide signs, knowing we are still grieving and needing assurance they are okay. That doesn't mean that your other pets don't give you signs. Because they know you have already dealt with their passing, their signs usually come mostly just around their birthday, adoption date or passing date.

What is a Visitation versus Dream?
Dreams are the easiest way for spirits to communicate. In dreams however, we may be able to see and hear someone in spirit, but we don't experience the feeling of touch like we do in visitations. Because Rhonda could feel her pets while her eyes were closed, it was not just a dream, but a visit. That's a much deeper experience, that often involves a tactile or scent sensation that feels real. Spirit visits require a lot more (emotional) energy than dream appearances. All those

animals wanted to let you know that they are always connected to you and are all together in spirit.

An Audible Visit

It takes a lot of energy for a spirit to speak, but Levin did exactly that, two weeks after he passed. Rhonda recalled that she awoke from a nap after hearing Levin purring on her pillow. She said he always loved to nap above her head on her pillow. She recalled, *"As I woke up, I heard him very clearly purring the way he did when he was super happy. I thought for a moment that one of my other kitties must have climbed up there and napped in his place. But as I looked up from my pillow to see who it was, there was no one there even though I'm certain of what I heard. I guess he was just happy to share one more nap with me and wanted me to know he was there."*

Once again, Levin provided a sign through a habit he had when he was in the physical: he would generate squeaking noises on the window. Pets usually provide signs through things they did when they were alive in the physical world, because they maintain the memories, personality, knowledge, and habits!

###

Chapter 21
Lucky Lou's Adele Message

One of the most common signs that spirits can send us are musical messages. In this chapter you'll read about a cat who was also paying attention to his mom's favorite music and let me know about it, as a message to her.

(Image: Lucky Lou listening intently. Credit: Tiffany)

Sometimes when you're driving your car you may turn on the radio at the exact time that a song plays that reminds you of a pet or person in spirit. That's not a coincidence. That was a spirit influencing you to turn the radio on to that exact station at that exact time, so you'll know they are with you. When pets do it, though, they also have help from a human in spirit.

As a medium, pets have shared or pointed out to me certain songs that only their pet parents associate with the spirit pet.

In my _Pets and the Afterlife 2 book_, you can read a story of a dog who insisted I tell his pet parent about Dolly Parton's #1 song, "I Will Always Love You," but specifically her 1983 version (she made 4 different recordings of it). His mom confirmed that is her favorite song and her favorite rendition, and it reminds her of her dog. It's not a coincidence.

Tiffany wrote me and said she asked her cat, Lucky Lou, to come into her dreams but had not yet received a sign. She noted that Lucky Lou's ashes came home two nights before, and she hoped that would enable Lucky Lou to come through. It seems, however, that Tiffany was still dealing with Lou's passing and had not yet worked through her grief. Grief blocks messages from spirit.

I responded in an email and explained that ashes contain some of our residual energies, so they do act as a small draw to spirit, but it's the bond of love we share that really connects us. Lucky Lou apparently influenced me to then write, "The most important thing to know is that it takes a lot of energy for a spirit to give us messages or say, 'Hello from the other side.'" I told her that although I wasn't purposely quoting Adele and her song, that popped into my head... and it was a message to Tiffany. I then explained that whenever she hears that song, she will know that Lucky Lou's spirit is right there with her.

Tiffany responded, _"Haha! I love Adele! Thank you! The pain has been so unbearable that I am so anxious for it to subside_ *so I can reconnect with her. She was with me for 18 years!"* Tiffany's next message was very telling.

A couple of hours later, Tiffany wrote me back and said, *"Wow, I got in the car to take the kids to a play. I never have regular radio on but when I fired up my car, guess what?!"* – *Tiffany attached a photo of her car radio, from right after she emailed me. When she started up the car and the radio went on, it was playing the Adele song, "Hello (from the other side)."*

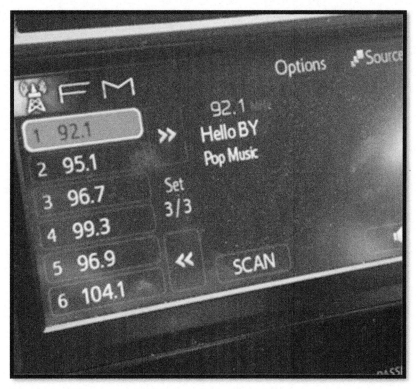

(Image: Tiffany took this photo after she got in her car and turned on her radio. It was playing Adele's "Hello" song. Credit: Tiffany M.)

She wrote, *"If you ever need a sign to put in your next book put her in there!*

When you told me about that song, I was putting my coat on to go out the door so it happened literally within 5 minutes. Maybe she intentionally brought me to your book!"

Spirits have a way of giving us very obvious signs even sometimes when our grief continues to block them out of our dreams. Lucky Lou worked through me as a medium to ensure that her mom got the message through a special song.

###

Chapter 22
The "Max from Uncle"

When anyone passes, whether human or animal, there are always spirits waiting to welcome us to the "other side." Spirits can be those of other people or animals. In Max's case, he immediately identified a certain uncle.

(Image: Max posing for the camera. Credit: Rocchina)

Rocchina wrote me for a reading with her cat Max who passed at 17 years old. She asked if I could connect with Max and find out from him if he is happy and feeling healthy and at peace where he is. She explained that her husband and son have been very upset since his passing and need to know how he is in spirit. When she emailed me, a photo of Max wasn't included. So, I had no idea what he looked like, and I wound up tapping into Max's energy through Rocchina's energy (although it's easier for me with a photo).

A Striped Tail and a Right Side
I wrote to Rocchina and told her first thing Max showed me was *"a somewhat striped cat tail curling around and perked up ears. Of course, I have no idea what he looked like. But he is safely on the other side."*

Max also showed me he liked to lay on his right side and expose his tummy. I told her "He's purring contentedly, too, telling me that he's grateful for the wonderful life he had with you and is still going to come around."

She confirmed the images that Max had conveyed. Rocchina wrote, *"Thank you so much for getting back to me and letting me know how Max is doing. I really appreciate it!! Max did have a striped tail. He was a short-haired domestic gray and white cat. Max did like lying on his right side on our carpet in the living room. I am so happy that is safely on the other side and that he is happy and purring and in perfect health."*

The "Max from Uncle"
Another unique and personal thing Max conveyed was his spirit company. I wrote Rocchina, "Was there someone that you referenced to him as 'uncle' who passed away? I keep hearing uncle... or is the 'uncle' someone that he particularly liked on this side? He seems quite connected to him."

Rocchina confirmed that her uncle had recently passed. She wrote, *"It is amazing that you said an uncle that passed away because my uncle Vince did pass away around a month ago. Thank you so much for getting back to me and confirming with me that Max is with my uncle Vince on the other side. This is truly amazing to hear.*

I am so grateful to you for connecting with Max. This really does bring comfort to my family and I."

***

Max provided proof that he was fine in spirit through conveying his habit of laying on his right side and showing me his striped tail (and I had no idea what he looked like). He also confirmed that he is being well cared for by an uncle who recently passed away.

As a side note, I couldn't resist making the title of this chapter a pun on the film and television series "A Man from U.N.C.L.E."

###

Chapter 23
Menagerie of Messages

Noëlle and her husband are loving pet parents who have had many pets pass. Noëlle shared with me experiences of her three cats and two family dogs. This chapter will help you identify many ways that spirit can communicate. You'll read different communications from Tommy, Floyd, Minou, Diane and Igor.

In 2016, Noëlle wrote me a detailed email about the passing of several pets over a period of several years. She allowed me to share her story in this chapter to help you understand different ways that your cats may be communicating with you. I also provided explanations. You'll read how each cat used a different means to communicate from the afterlife.

Noëlle wrote, *"I just wanted to say that I found your email address in your book "Pets and the Afterlife 2" which brought me much comfort. I thank you very much for that. In a year's time, I've lost 3 out of 4 best friends (fur friends).*

I was very sad when I lost (my cat) Minou on May 20, 2015, and then Tommy on July 30, 2015 (they were 2 adorable cats). So, I started looking for answers on the Internet concerning an afterlife for our animal friends. On April 14, 2016, I found a video broadcast about a year ago on YouTube in which we hear you talk on Paranormal zone TV. You were

Norene Balovich's guest. During the interview, you talked about signs from our pets on the other side, like finding pennies, among other things."

(Image: Tommy, the white tabby cat in August of 2008. Credit: Noëlle N.)

Tommy's Coin

"The next day, April 15, 2016, as I was walking home from work, I asked my deceased cat Tommy to please send me a sign that he was okay by putting a coin with his birth year on it on my path. In about less than 3 minutes I found a shiny yellow 10 cents with the year 2000 on it! I was so glad..."

Signs from Tommy Hinting at Floyd's Passing

Sometimes a spirit can send us signs to prepare us or "warn" us that someone may pass. In this case, Tommy in spirit forewarned Noëlle and her husband about Floyd's condition.

Noëlle wrote, *"Before Floyd's passing, I have noticed a few weird things. Before his death, as I was walking home, I met a cat that reminded me a lot of my parents' cat who passed away in December 2006. Another day (still before Floyd's death), almost at the same spot was a sleeping cat that looked much like Floyd."*

The first cat was a sign that one of her other cats may soon pass. Seeing a look-alike in almost the same spot was another clue as to which pet it would be whom passed.

Floyd Passes
Noëlle wrote, *"On that same day (I found the coin from Tommy) in the evening, I noticed that my beloved Floyd (my 3rd cat) was unwell. With my husband we decided to take him to the vet the following Monday and everything seemed alright.*

But Floyd was not eating much and seemed to save his strength by remaining all day on the sofa. We then decided to take him to the vet again. This time he underwent an echography and an X-ray of his chest which revealed that he had lung cancer and not much long to live, a few months at the most.

(Photo: The grey tabby cat is Floyd. This picture was taken in September 2015. Credit: Noëlle N.)

I was devastated at the news. In fact, even the palliative treatment didn't work, and he was neither eating nor drinking anymore by himself. We had to give him fluids with a pipette. I was crying most of the time because I couldn't bear to see him like this and because I knew he was going to leave us soon.

I said to myself, 'Why him, why now?' At some point, we had to make the final decision I had always dreaded...On Friday, 13th May 2016 we went one last time to the vet to put an end to his suffering.

Since then, I keep wondering if my cat Tommy put this coin on my path the very same day Floyd was beginning to show the signs of his illness to give me hope and strength for all that was to come..."

Floyd's Dream Appearance

Noëlle wrote, *"Since Floyd's passing, I have dreamt of him twice getting on our bed but not seeming alright. Perhaps this was not a sign of him and rather my imagination, but I am worried about him."*

Two Past Pets Make a Special Spirit "Visit"

A visit is a much deeper experience than a dream. A visit is a dream where you see and actually hear, smell, or feel the pet or person who has passed. Noëlle received those deep visits from two pets who had passed long before.

Noëlle noted, *"After his (Floyd's) passing, I've also dreamt of (my cat) Minou sleeping in my lap, and of Diane (my father's deceased dog) who was pushing her nose under my right arm. This felt so real...that I woke up!"*

Another Childhood Dog Comes Through

When our pets pass, they reunite with all the other pets associated with us during any time in our lives. Sometimes when a pet recently passes, they will give us a sign that

118

they're with another pet from our past. That's what happened after Floyd's passing. Noëlle's husband's childhood dog had a human spirit help to ensure that a calendar was opened to a certain page, and that Noëlle would sit next to it and see it.

Noëlle said, *"Then, Floyd's death made my husband talk about a dog he had when he was little. His parents had to give him away to another family after he had spent a few years with them. My husband was sad because he thought his parents didn't give Igor (that was his dog's name) the life he deserved.*

The next morning, when I arrived at work, I was asked to move to another desk (which was not planned), and on it was a block calendar open at June 5th, St. Igor... On the same day my husband met a dog in the street that was the spitting image of Igor."

Floyd Uses a Toy and Electricity

If they have enough energy, spirits can move objects, like toys, and manipulate electrical things because they are beings of energy with a consciousness. They can also hear us because sound and thoughts are energy, and they are energy. So, if you make a request, they can acknowledge it if they have enough energy to do so.

Noëlle wrote, *"To end my story, the other evening I said to my husband thinking out loud 'Where might be Floyd now?' and my husband said, 'Floyd, could you give us a sign please?' And a few minutes later, my daughter's talking doll (which was in her bedroom and hadn't been touched for quite a while) began to talk on its own, as we were all 3 of us in the living room. And right after that, a light bulb in the living room burned out!"*

(Photo Noëlle's daughter's talking doll that spoke by itself from the other room after she and her husband asked for a sign from the spirit cat, Floyd. Credit: N.N.)

All of the strange things that Noëlle and her husband experienced were messages from spirits of their various pets. When it comes to spirit, there is no such thing as a coincidence.

###

Chapter 24
Misty's Look-Alikes

Mhairi's cats Misty and Harley left home one night and never returned. Mhairi sensed that Misty had crossed over. She received a couple of signs that helped confirm her feelings. She also felt that Misty had a hand in bringing her two other cats needing homes.

(Photo: Misty on a lamp. Credit: M.M.)

Misty's Spirit Sends a Look-Alike on an Anniversary
Mhairi told me she was reading my Pets and the Afterlife 2 book and it helped make her aware of signs from spirits. She noted it was coming up on a year since she last saw Misty and thought she heard Misty (in spirit) jump in the window one night but there was no one there. She also said, *"I'm sure I've*

heard his meow and purr, so I think it's safe to say he is in spirit. I am not sure about Harley, most of my instincts tell me she's alive and cared for." I told Mhairi that I also didn't get the sense that Harley had passed as I couldn't sense her in spirit.

Misty's Spirit Brings 2 Cats
Mhairi explained that she was "adopted" by two cats that were abandoned and looking for shelter and she was grateful they choose her. She questioned if they were guided to her. I explained that spirits often guide us to the next pet or pets they would like us to adopt, so Misty did bring her those two cats. Spirits will do that because they want living animals to get the chance to experience the same wonderful feeling of love they did.

Misty's Spirit Sends a Look-Alike on an Anniversary
Weeks later, Mhairi wrote me after the first-year anniversary of Misty's and Harley's disappearances. She said she had reviewed again the events of their disappearance and was blaming herself for not doing enough to find them.

Around the anniversary of their disappearance, she said, *"My mum called me into my garden because there was a strange cat, and it hadn't run from her dog. It was a tabby that could well have been Misty's twin, just sitting calmly. He wasn't my little man, he was smaller and not neutered, but he had the same markings and coloring, and he would've let me pet him if my two current cats hadn't come out. There was growling and posturing, and he backed off. I did manage to give him some treats and even called him Misty, but it wasn't him.*

The fact he didn't run from the dog and stayed close to my garden even though Diva and Barley (her other cats) clearly wanted him to leave, makes me wonder if he was there to convey some message. I had been thinking about him more than usual due to the significance of the date and the memory of the loss and search."

Spirits usually give us signs on anniversaries, which in this case was the one-year anniversary of Misty's disappearance and ultimately passing. The appearance of the look-alike was the doing of Misty's spirit. Misty's spirit led a doppelganger cat to Mhairi. Misty also helped Mhairi the two new cats she would adopt. These are two common things that spirits do for us to let us know they are still very much around us.

*****

Another Doppelganger Years Later
In 2019, Mhairi moved to a flat (apartment) two streets from her previous address. Both Misty and Harley had been missing since 2016 and the two cats who adopted her after their disappearance were both settled with her. She recalled, *"After moving in, while enjoying a cup of tea in the garden, another silver tabby with a collar trotted up with its tail in the air, meowing at me. He let me pet him for a few minutes, rubbing himself around my legs. He was not Misty, but I took it as another message from him all the same. I had never met this cat before nor have I seen it since.*

[My two living cats] Barley and Diva never met him (the visiting silver tabby) as they were both shut indoors at the time. They are still comfortable with me and I love them both dearly. I am grateful to them for choosing to stay with me while I was in need of comfort after the loss of Misty and Harley. I am glad I was able to offer them a home when they were in need of one."

###

Chapter 25
Nala's Yellow Bird and Spirit Family

After Kelsey's cat, Nala, passed at 18 years, she wrote me to get a reading and see if Nala had anything to convey from spirit. Nala confirmed her illness, provided multiple names of family members in spirit and told of a special "yellow bird," all of which made sense to Kelsey. This is Nala's story.

(Photo: Nala resting. Credit: Kelsey)

Nala's Many Messages
I connected with Nala on Feb. 13, 2022, and the first thing she said to me was "My house!" Nala told me that she was in 2 houses (that she remembers), but the house Kelsey was in (before she passed) was her favorite house. That was the first time a pet told me they liked a certain house.

Kelsey confirmed Nala's message and said, *"It warms my heart to know how much she loves this house, I always tell everyone how she was happiest here."*

Nala's Physical Sharing

Pets sometimes share the physical pain they endured before they passed or a significant pain that occurred during their lifetime (as a human would if they break a leg). It's their way to help identify them.

Nala made me feel kidney issues and a heaviness in the stomach... like there was an urge to urinate. Then she conveyed just feeling weak. I told Kelsey that Nala would feel "weak as a kitten." She also felt badly about missing the litter box. That stuck with her because she says she couldn't help it. Kelsey confirmed, *"You were spot on about the kidney failure."*

The Spirit Family of Greeters

During the reading, I shared what Nala showed me in my mind. I wrote to Kelsey that once Nala crossed into the light, there were several people waiting for her.

She gave me the names James/Jim, Robert/Bobby; Ann or Andrea (something that sounds like it begins with "An"). I explained that Nala said there are grandparents and a young child who passed (it could be a miscarriage who is appearing as a young child). There were also two other cats in the light. One cat had similar colorations to Nala, and the other appeared to be orange.

Confirming all the Spirits

Kelsey was able to identify all of the spirits that Nala said that she was with on the other side. Kelsey wrote, *"Jim was my great grandpa. My mom had a brother, Bobby, who only lived for a few hours after birth. And my grandpa's name was*

Robert. I also have a deceased aunt and great aunt with the middle name 'Ann.' So incredible, I can't thank you enough!"

Nala's Yellow Bird

When spirits connect with me, they sometimes make me see images or events from my past experiences that relate to them. That's what happened with the next amazing message.

I wrote to Kelsey: "Nala is mentioning a yellow bird. That could be a toy or perhaps a real bird- but she'll use a "yellow bird" as a sign she's around, too. It could be something you see on-line, in person, in a book, etc. She showed me Snoopy's friend Woodstock to indicate it's a yellow bird."

On my Weimaraner Dolly's, last day in Oct. 2020, she spent most of the day laying on her bed with her head propped up on a stuffed Peanuts yellow Woodstock toy. Now, when I hold it, I feel like I'm hugging my Dolly in spirit.

Kelsey understood Nala's message about the yellow bird. She wrote, *"The yellow bird thing blows my mind. After she passed, I framed a photo of her and put two ceramic yellow birds next to it. I just want you to know how spot on you were and how much it means to me!*

Thank you so much for communicating with Nala and taking the time to detail it for me with such precision. I shared the email with my mom and it brought her a lot of comfort, too."

Nala's Audible Afterlife Purr

After the reading, Kelsey shared an audible sign that her mom received from Nala. She wrote, *"The evening my mom got to our house and found Nala had passed, my in-laws came over and helped give her a proper burial. My mom said she woke up in bed the next morning to the sound of Nala's purring right*

That was Nala's way of letting Kelsey's mom
ad safely crossed over.

###

Chapter 26
Nemo's Fish and Other Confirmations

Nemo is a black cat with white fur on his chest and face. He passed in 2017 and his dad, Brian requested a reading to check that he was okay in spirit and if was okay with the decision made to help him pass. Nemo provided affirmative answers to both, but shared other things that let his dad know he is around in spirit.

Nemo's Physical Sensations

Nemo conveyed appreciation for being so loved and well-cared for, and or "letting him do his thing." Then as I was communicating with Nemo's spirit, he suddenly decided to share his physical feelings before his passing. He made me feel as if he had some kidney issues (made me feel like I had to go to the bathroom), and he was sorry he missed the litter box a few times.

Brian confirmed the kidney issue and missing the litter box. Brian wrote, *"The kidney issues/missing the litter box does make sense. Shortly before he passed, we found out he was in the mid-stages of renal failure. I also had to watch the type of food that I fed him as if I didn't use a urinary tract specific food, he would start having issues going to the bathroom. Once I switched to that food, and later went on an all-wet food diet, it really helped, and it was minimal when he missed the box after that. But it did happen a few times."*

Messages about Passing and a Carrier

Then Nemo addressed the end of his time. I told Brian that Nemo understood when he had to make the decision because Nemo knew his body wasn't cooperating. Although Nemo couldn't figure out what was happening to himself, he knew he didn't like it. He also started to feel really tired, very lethargic.

Nemo then addressed the transportation to the vet. He told me he was vocal about going in a carrier to go to the vet. He was a little claustrophobic, thus, not liking the carrier. However, he did convey that he was okay with the decision to help him cross over.

Brian replied, *"And yes; he really did not like going in a kennel. I would have taken him to the vet more often, but it stressed him out so much; I really did not like putting him through that. And related to the day of his passing, we had a pretty bad experience with the doctor at the emergency vet. He was very "cold" about the whole situation and made it worse, which left me second guessing my decision that day to let him pass. It's very comforting to know he was OK with it and is at peace."*

A Special Fish and the New Office
The next two messages from Nemo really struck Brian and confirmed that Nemo's spirit is still visiting.

At the end of the reading, I told Brian that Nemo has been visiting as a quick-moving shadow in the house, especially near the office door and he keeps saying the word "office." He also mentioned that he's been up on a desk and has accidentally put some papers on the floor while walking around in spirit. Nemo showed me a special fish. So, I wrote Brian, "Do you have a fish-shaped toy of his? He's talking about it. If you have one, please just set it near his picture." It felt like there was a request or connection between "fish" and "picture."

Brian's response to these messages included the photo of a special painting. Brian wrote, *"I wanted to share with you a photo of a painting I had made by an artist friend of mine, shortly after Nemo passed in 2017. I told her to use her artistic judgement and she certainly did. I'm a drummer, and she incorporated a drumstick (as a fishing pole) with an orange fish (see attached). It hangs over my desk; in my office.*

(Painting of Nemo by: Jennifer M. Jackson Fine Art & Commissions theartgoddess@gmail.com/ www.facebook.com/ArtGoddessStudios)

It's crazy to me that Nemo knows about my office because I have moved since he passed. Where we lived before, I didn't have an office and did my work at the kitchen table. Since I've moved, I now have an office which is where I spend most of my time. It's comforting to know that he found me after the move.

Thank you so much for this. Words can't express my gratitude that you provide this service to so many, and at such an affordable price. Just saying "thank you" doesn't seem adequate but I really, truly appreciate this, Rob."

###

Chapter 27
O'Kitty Grieves, Spirit Sent A Living Cat

This chapter is unique because it's not about messages from a spirit cat, but instead shows how our living pets grieve the loss of their companions, and how a human spirit influenced a mysterious cat to appear to convey she was fine in spirit.

In 2018, Jeanne and her family experienced a lot of loss. Her sister-in-law passed. Her horse passed and then two of her beloved dogs passed.

(Photo: O'Kitty and CC. Credit: Jeanne)

Spirit Sends a Special Cat Messenger
Jeanne explained that the spirit of her sister-in-law brought a mysterious cat to her and her husband. The spirit chose a cat because she was a cat mom in life.

Jeanne wrote, *"Recently my sister-in-law passed, and the next morning a friendly, but strange, orange tabby showed up in our garage. He was very loving and wanted my husband and I to pet and hold him. We contacted our neighbors to see if he was roaming from home (we have a lot of owls, coyotes, and eagles around), but no one claimed him. Thinking he was a stray we fed him and figured he would be back for more food.*

We never saw him again, and my husband is sure it was his sister saying goodbye - she was a 'kitty mom' who rescued and fed many strays. She had always wanted a golden tabby but all the cats that came to her were calicos, greys, or blacks."

Jeanne's sister-in-law's spirit worked hard to get a message that she was okay and conveying it through the feral orange tabby. People and pets in spirit can influence animals to make appearances, stare at us or act oddly as a sign they are around.

***

A Literal Sign from Above
Before or after our pets pass, we can ask them to send us a sign they are okay. Often, they send us a particular sign associated with something they were familiar with in life. It could be influencing a bird to behave oddly in front of us. They could drop a coin, or even send a "thunderstorm," in this case!

Jeanne noted that after her 26-year-old horse passed, she read my "Pets and the Afterlife 2" book. Jeanne's horse came to her family when the horse was just three years old, and they formed a good bond.

She recalled that she asked her horse to send her a little "thunderstorm" as a sign she reached the other side and was

134

okay. She recalled, *"Well, a few hours later we had not a little storm, but a horrendous storm with tornado warnings. I told her she made her point and could back off a bit. The storm finished quickly and uneventfully shortly after."*

Cats Grieve Loss Like We Do

The thunderstorm reminded Jeanne of when she said goodbye to two senior dogs: LT the husky and CC the Labrador retriever, were best friends and both in ill health. They were buried together in Jeanne's backyard, and she said *"We lined it with hay and their blankets, added their favorite toys and placed wildflowers over them.*

Then we noticed that there were two bird wings laying on the edge of the site. Our cat, O'Kitty, brought his friends some wings to help them on their journey! I placed one wing on each of them." That was O'Kitty's acknowledgement of their passing.

(Photo: LT, CC, and their best buddy - O'Kitty (middle). Credit: Jeanne)

Soon, thunderstorms moved in, and everyone went inside. Jeanne thought it ironic that a thunderstorm rolled by when both dogs were afraid of them. She then had a realization and said, *"I looked at my husband and said, 'I guess the girls are letting us know they made it over the bridge and aren't afraid of lightning anymore'! It did bring us some peace."*

Meanwhile, O'Kitty continued to grieve after acknowledging LT and CC's passing. Jeanne said O'Kitty continued to sit by the grave site for months afterward, communing in some way with his friends. O'Kitty experienced the same sense of intense grief and loss that Jeanne and her husband did. When our pets suffer a loss, they also need more comfort and attention, until they can begin to accept the passings of other pets.

###

Chapter 28
New Zealand's Po Gives Clear Messages

Po is a special cat from New Zealand who changed the lives of his parents, Nick and Charlotte. His short time in the physical was filled with love and a very special bond between him and his pet parents. After Po passed, his dad reached out to me for a reading and many of Po's messages resonated. This chapter is about those messages.

Nick wrote me asking just a few questions and Po came back with a number of messages. Nick asked if Po was okay and said he can still feel Po's love. He asked if there was some way Po would like to connect with him and if Po had anything to say.

Smart, and Acting like a Dog
Po came through clearly and conveyed that he is quite smart, smarter than the average cat, and of course very curious. He gave me the feeling that he was somewhat trained and acted more like a dog than a cat.

Nick confirmed Po's intelligence and dog-like behavior. Nick said, *"He was the smartest cat I have ever known he was more like a dog than a cat. He would follow me everywhere much like a dog would and just loved to be doing whatever you were doing. He was very social around other animals and people. We trained him to play fetch with his toys. He was so quirky and brought us so many laughs."*

(Image: Po, dressed up for the holidays. Credit; N.H)

Spirit Company

Po mentioned two people he is with in spirit, one was a man named "Randy" or "Andy" but Nick couldn't place him. He could be a distant relative or childhood friend who had an affinity for cats. The other was a woman there that Po called "mum." I explained that it is a woman who is 2 generations older than Nick and Charlotte (likely a grandmother), and on his or her father's side. Po conveyed "'Mum' was rounding people up, liked big feasts and cooked for many. She still welcomes everyone in spirit, including cats, dogs, and other critters." It sounds like Po has a lot of company in spirit.

Nick identified the woman. He said, *"I'm very sure the 'mum' grandmother you have mentioned is my partner's grandmother. She was like a mother to my partner Charlotte and was mainly known for cooking excessive large feasts at any chance she could get. Apparently, she would do it daily and it was her way of love. She lived on a farm so I'm sure there's plenty of animals with him."*

Po's Self-made "Cat Door"
Po shared with me that he loved the freedom allowed him. He felt like he "ran" the house because he could go wherever he wanted. He showed me what looked like a small door to the outside he would go in and out of, so I asked Nick if they had a cat/dog door.

Nick confirmed that Po made his own "cat door to the outside." He wrote, *"We moved into Charlotte's Aunt's very large Edwardian house [and Po] did run through the house and ended up having so much freedom there. We noticed him coming in and out of the kitchen window - it was a small opening that was held by a latch (that resembled a small door to the outside). We ended up always making sure the kitchen sliding window was open for him all day and night. He was the first one of our cats to use it and almost taught the others of this entry. He would come in and out during the night it was kind of his door."*

Po Mentions His Nighttime Visits
Po mentioned he would be around the house during the day or evening from time to time, and he would make an

appearance in Nick and Charlotte's dreams over a couple of weeks. But he told me he had already given another sign to them when he jumped on their bed at night and was the soft feeling of pressure against him.

(Image: Nick is an artist in Australia, and he painted this portrait of Po on his shoulder, to memorialize Po. Credit: Nick Herd)

Nick confirmed Po's daytime and nighttime visits. Nick wrote, *"That's amazing you said that! I wanted to badly ask you in the first email if that was him that jumped on the bed softly* walked up my legs and rested on me. I knew it was him. I feel crazy telling people this. It woke me up and really felt like him. It made me feel so good I cried in joy It was the most bizarre thing I felt like he was telling me he was ok; I could just feel the love we had so intensely. I've never had that happen to me. I have also seen him in my dreams a few times too It was really lovely.

Out of the bottom of my Heart THANK YOU so much. I can see how this must bring you so much Joy helping others. Reading your book has also helped me so much. It has opened my eyes and mind to something I would have never thought. I have been missing everything about him and grieving so intensely. He is my baby boy and my world I spent so much time daily with him and getting to learning that we are still connected and that there's not just an end to it - just has opened a whole new world to me."

Honoring Po in a Painting

Nick Herd is an artist who concentrates on his personal relationships and experiences to create his richly colored, textured paintings. After Po passed, he was inspired to memorialize him in a self-portrait with Po on his shoulder.

Creating a painting, drawing, scrapbook, getting a tattoo, or crocheting a throw or making a tee shirt with your pet's image on it are great ways to honor them. It not only keeps their memories alive, but it makes us feel closer to them even though they are in spirit.

###

More About Nick Herd: Painting from life, Herd captures the sensitive nature and complexity of his subjects; each work gritty and saturated with information. Herd's use of color is kept loose and is in constant evolution. Excited by how different colors interact, he is continually seeking new relationships. Herd's work is characterized by expressionistic mark making and unrefined, sometimes grotesque, figurative depiction.

His love for the physicality, the substance of paint and mark making marry together to form a visual and emotive field of color. With references to modernism's Neo-Expressionism and contemporary faux naïf Herd is interested in painting as a physical discharge of energy and anxiety. The model or still life become vessels for thoughtful meditation in his attempts to communicate a human experience to the viewer.

For more information, visit: www.nickherd.com

###

Chapter 29
Rhumba and Butthead: 2 Active Spirit Cats

Rhumba and Butthead were two bonded cats who lived with Christopher and his wife. Rhumba preceded Butthead in passing and I connected with Rhumba in spirit who gave me signs. When Butthead passed, he provided two blunt visible signs directly to his parents.

Rhumba's Reading
In 2016, Christopher wrote and asked me to connect with Rhumba. He said, *"I got to know of you when I watched Ms. Norene Balovich's Paranormal TV "Animals in Heaven: Do Pets Have Souls?" recently. I want to tell you that your words have brought a lot of comfort to me and my wife as we had just lost our 12 years old beloved cat Rhumba on Tuesday, September 20th."*

When I did connect with Rhumba, he told me about his unique voice, his visits and who was with him in spirit.

Rhumba said as a spirit, he was walking around the legs of an older man, someone like grandfatherly figure. I saw boots on the man, and a vehicle, like someone who worked in a farming job, outside.

Christopher was able to identify two men who fit Rhumba's description. *"As for the elderly man, I can only think of two possible persons: My uncle (my father's younger brother) or my wife's grandfather; both worked for the forestry and agricultural department with their respective government (my uncle with Malaysia and my wife's grandfather was with the Burmese side). I however have never met my wife's grandfather."*

We need not have met someone on the other side for them to take care of our pets. Usually, those people have an affinity for animals, which is why they come forward. It makes sense that someone who worked in an outdoor profession would have more of a love for animals.

(Image: Rhumba. Credit: C.T.)

Rhumba told me that he had already and quickly visited his home and that Butthead had already seen him in spirit.

Christopher confirmed his other cats likely saw Rhumba visiting. *"Recalling back to the time almost immediately after Rhumba's passing (I believe it was the second day) I did notice strange and odd behavior by my cats, including*

Butthead. They would look and stare at places (most of it were Rhumba's favorite spots – chair, the big pet cushion on the floor etc.) - like as if something was there. I wasn't sure what to make of it then but now I know it was Rhumba visiting."

Another thing that stood out during my connection with Rhumba in spirit was that he said he had a distinct "meow."

Christopher confirmed the message about Rhumba's voice. He said, *"Yes, Mr. Gutro you heard Rhumba right on! Rhumba has a unique voice, unlike any typical cat!*

Your words give us so much comfort for where Rhumba is, however we are now facing a battle to save my other cat's life. His name is Butthead. The doctors list his survival on day-to-day basis. We are so distraught over such a turn of events. His kidney is failing, he has just developed pancreatitis and just today the doctor began worrying of his weakening heart as so much IV fluids were given to him. We are so stricken by grief, faced with long odds in keeping Butthead alive. We are just so numb about the whole thing now."

Butthead's Passing
On Sept 30, Christopher emailed me and told me Butthead passed away in his arms at noon from cardiac arrest. He said, *"His passing comes just 10 days after Rhumba's. Butthead's struggle is over, and I hope my two boys are now reunited."*

Recognizing Rhumba Waiting, and Butthead's Early Signs
Christopher's next email on the next day clearly showed several signs from Rhumba who had passed earlier that month. He recognized Rhumba's spirit was waiting for Butthead, he saw Rhumba in spirit, and he felt the spirit of Butthead on him in bed at the exact time Butthead had passed the day before (that's how he knew it was Butthead visiting).

Christopher continued, *"Thank you, Mr. Gutro. I am learning so much from watching you over You Tube. It is remarkable that I am grieving a lot less in Butthead's passing as compared to that of Rhumba's. What you have said about their spirits being around us and the signs from the other cats is so true."*

Christopher continued: *"Several things happened after their passing (especially after Rhumba) that is so remarkable:*

(Image: Butthead. Credit: C.T)

1) On several occasions my cats including Butthead stares at places as if Rhumba was still around

2) I thought I caught a glimpse of a cat dashing by just two nights after Rhumba's passing

3) Just two nights before Butthead's death, I was at the STVS hospital cradling Butthead after a seizure (when the doctor permitted him out of the oxygen room briefly), Butthead on one occasion looked intently at a corner of a room as if looking at someone and even called out....I think that was Rhumba!

4) Just today, Oct. 1, when I took short late morning nap, I felt the weight and warmth of a cat between my legs and I think that was Butthead and when I woke up the weight and warmth slowly disappeared and when I looked at the clock it was 12pm, the time of Butthead's passing the day earlier! I am actually so comforted by those signs."

Butthead's Spirit Presence Within 9 Days

On Oct 9, Christopher wrote me to share more good news of signs. He said, *"Butthead is making his presence known! My wife caught a glimpse of him from the corner of her eyes just last night after she got back from her long work abroad.*

Just three days back I found my bed comforters in a mess…just like what Butthead used to do when he was alive, younger, energetic and happy…he would just jump around the bed and mess up the comforters. Unless my mind was playing tricks but I think that was what he just did. I sure was happy seeing that!"

A Note of Thanks

I enjoyed reading Christopher's note knowing that he and his wife were comforted by the signs they acknowledged from their two cats who passed ten days apart: *"You can't imagine how much you have been a blessing to us at this crucial point in time. Once more, thank you for your help. You have an extraordinary gift and your use of that gift to help those in need is such a blessing and comforting. God bless you Mr. Gutro."*

###

Chapter 30
Snobee's Spirit Shares Several Signs

Thea was reeling on May 1, 2021, after the passing of her 14-year-old beautiful cat Snobee. She wrote me from the Philippines, where she said Snobee was her source of inspiration, strength, and comfort over the course of their time together. Thea felt lost, as many pet parents do when their best friend passes. She reached out to me hoping to get some acknowledgement that Snobee was already on the other side, but she didn't expect that Snobee would provide a special number, reveal who was with her in the afterlife, and even talk about a special bird!

After connecting to Snobee through her photograph, I wrote Thea with all the messages (and there were many) that Snobee provided. Thea replied, *"Thank you for your response. I was reading your email with joyful tears as I confirm the details you mentioned."*

Here's what Snobee had to share:

Numbers and Birthdate

Thea sent me a photo of Snobee on her last birthday on April 19. She only knew Snobee was born in April and didn't know the day, and I later learned Thea assigned her birthdate of April 19th to Snobee so they would share it.

However, during the reading, Snobee provided the exact date of her birth. She kept showing me the number 17. Snobee said April 17 was her actual birthdate. She was smiling, and said she was honored to have Thea's birthdate, nevertheless. I relayed to Thea that the numbers 1 and 7, or 17 or 71 will be important signs from Snobee.

(Photo: Snobee and Thea from their last sunset photoshoot from the rooftop of her building. Credit: Thea)

Whenever she sees those numbers — whether a house number, in a time on the clock, or something else — she should be reminded that Snobee is around her. Thea responded, *"It was such a surprising revelation to know that her actual birthday is on April 17. I will keep the numbers 17, 1, 7, and 71 close to my heart. In fact, my family's house number in the province is #7 and my place in the city is #307. It was definitely my pleasure to have shared the same birthdate with her for 14 years, though."*

Snobee's Afterlife Company

I confirmed that Snobee had crossed over into the light, and told Thea there was a motherly figure waiting there to greet her. The woman was wearing an ankle-length dress and an apron; she was wearing glasses and wore her dark haired pulled back. She welcomed Snobee to the other side. Thea confirmed the spirit. She said, *"Yes, that was my grandmother (she passed away 2 years ago) who welcomed my Snobee to the other side. In fact, the dress you described was what she wore in her casket. She was fond of dogs and cats, and I could just imagine her delight in welcoming Snobee. Knowing that they're together now brings me so much peace."*

Messages of Love With Some Humor

Our pets in spirit always convey the love they shared with their parents, and Snobee was no exception. Snobee acknowledged the last birthday celebration Thea gave her. I told Thea that Snobee liked her cake, although she didn't know what to make of it. She said she sensed Thea's happiness during her birthday and that made her feel so special. She said she lived a wonderful life and couldn't have asked for a better one.

Snobee loves her mom with all her heart. She said she will continue to inspire Thea from spirit and would act as a guide to take her to places and do things that will give her peace.

(Photo: Snobee celebrating a birthday. Credit: Thea)

In addition, Snobee mentioned she will lead Thea to find a cat that resembles her. Sometimes our pets have special requests when it comes to our adoption of another pet. Snobee had one of those requests. She told me she will lead Thea to adopt another cat, but she wants her to adopt a male cat because she wants to be the only female cat in her life. I told Thea that Snobee has a good sense of humor.

Thea replied, *"I always make sure to make her birthdays special, but the last one was the most memorable. We had our sunset photoshoot, and I got her a beautiful cake. Little did I know that would be her last one. I'm in tears knowing how much she loves me and how I made her short life wonderful the best way I know how.*

I'm looking forward to her guiding me in spirit, going places and attaining peace. I'm not quite ready to have another cat but will make sure to get a male one when I do. And yes, my Snobee is a funny and jealous cat. How I miss her so."

Footsteps on the Floors and Favorite Spot

Right after Snobee crossed over she started walking on the wooden floors in Thea's house. Snobee said she would sit in her favorite place where there's a beam of sunlight near it. In addition, she said she would lay against Thea at night (a slight pressure will be felt), but it will be against her feet (not legs, which is usually what cats tell me — Snobee wants to be different). Thea confirmed the floors and her favorite spot. *"Yes, I have wooden floors where she spent her lazy days and her lounge area in front of my bed has a beam of sunlight. I will be keeping that spot for her. She also has a pillow on the edge of my bed where she likes to rest, that's probably why you mentioned she'll stay near my feet. And at night, she would be on top of my pillow as we doze off to sleep together."*

Snobee's Bird

Snobee showed me the image of a yellow or orange bird. It seemed to be important to her. I asked if it was a toy or a live bird. She seemed to have been fascinated with a bird, and as a spirit, will also use birds to get her attention. I instructed Thea to watch out for birds that act oddly, and that's how she will know Snobee is influencing them. Whenever the bird or birds are there, Snobee's presence will also be felt.

Astonishingly, Thea confirmed Snobee's bird. She said, *"That bird she showed you is actually our favorite bird perched on my balcony every morning. My Snobee was diabetic, and I would feed and inject her with insulin every 8:30am, and then feed the birds afterwards. She loved watching the birds from the dining table. There are several of them, mostly blue/gray pigeons, but there's this brown/orange one that is so unique and special to us. I will continue looking after the birds and watch out for Snobee's signs among them. I'm in tears right now as I am comforted with the assurance that Snobee will still be with me every morning in spirit through our birds."*

Those were amazing number of signs from Snobee. She proved how much she was aware of her environment and the other side. Thea said, *"I do appreciate the comforting information you have shared, Rob. I'm not sure when my grieving ends, or if it ever will, but the void in my heart is filled with peace knowing that my Snobee is now with my grandma; that I have made her life on earth wonderful; and that she will always be with me in spirit."*

###

Chapter 31
Wooster's "Cat's Eye's Opal" and more

Wooster is an incredibly communicative feline in spirit and provided an amazing number of messages for his dad, Paul. After I emailed Wooster's reading, Paul wrote back with quite a few confirmations. This chapter is a good example of all the things that your cat notices in life and can convey in spirit.

In March 2022, Paul booked a reading for his black cat, Wooster. He said his cat's name was originally spelled "Worcester," but he spelled it phonetically as it sounds the same. Paul heard my interview on the "Unsolved Mysteries" podcast and said, *"I was so moved I had to look up your website and get your books and book this reading."*

(Photo: Wooster. Credit: Paul Y.)

Paul provided a couple of photos, noted 2 people in the household and had four questions that included who his spirit company is, how will he give signs, is there someone else he misses, and is he attached to the building or to Paul.

When I connected with Wooster, and before I even got to address Paul's questions, Wooster started talking and said a lot! Wooster was able to answer all the questions and more!

Recognized "Spoiled" and the Other Man

The first thing Wooster told me was "He is grateful to you both for a very comfortable and 'spoiled' life! - He said 'spoiled,' so he's heard the word before. Who is the other living man that Wooster is very fond of?"

Paul said, *"The word 'spoiled' is one Wooster's original 'Mama' (who passed away and that's how we got him) would use, as would her husband and friends as she really doted over him. And when I got him, I completely spoiled and worshipped him (it actually made my boyfriend jealous at times, LOL!). And that's who the other man is that Wooster was very fond of - they were buddies and play pals. But with me, Wooster was so gentle, and we had a much closer bond that was deep."*

Pet Spirits Can Hear Us

As my connection with Wooster continued, he told me Paul was emotionally hit hard when he passed, and he has been giving signs of his presence to help Paul understand he's okay. Wooster told me that Paul has talked to him from time to time, especially right after he passed. He could hear everything Paul said and he reaffirmed his love for Paul.

Paul confirmed, *"It's true, I was devastated when Wooster died. It made me question everything I believed in, and it broke my trust in a Higher Power for a few months. I've lost* family and friends, but nothing left me so gutted as when he got sick and died. I still talk to him and tell him in my prayers every night and I'm glad he can hear me."

Ashes and "Cat's Eye Opal"

My chat with Wooster's Spirit next addressed his remains and a special stone. I wrote to Paul, "Do you have his ashes? He's telling me about a box, which I assume are his ashes. And he's showing me his photos around your house. Now he's telling me about some kind of stone - something that has significance to him. (I keep hearing "Cat's eye opal" for some reason) but there's special stone he's talking about."

Paul responded, *"I do have his ashes, right on my desk to my right and it is surrounded by really vibrant blue labradorite rocks, chunks of rainbows and blue hues from the labradorite all around his little 'altar' and box. I used to put some of them in his cat bed the last months of his life, I think that's what the 'Cat's Eye's Opal' you mentioned. That is completely accurate, and I don't think I've ever told anyone else about that. Thank you so much."*

Wooster's Specific Spot

Every cat has their favorite spot to lounge, sleep, or sun. Wooster said his was a spot under a table [where] he liked curling up, and on the top of a chair or couch.

Paul confirmed, *"I know exactly where those spots are under the table you mentioned (I actually hung butterflies made of feathers above his cat bed that was under my desk) and that's where he really liked being at, especially at the end of his life."*

Wooster's Spirit Company

Wooster identified at least four people in spirit who are with him. I wrote, "The first was a man named Mike or Michael, who could be a relative or someone either of you know who passed, and likely had an affinity for animals. There are three mother figures in spirit - they could be mother or grandmothers." I also conveyed what Wooster told me about their personalities and their hobbies.

Paul understood Wooster's spirit company. He confirmed, *"We have a neighbor a few floors above us who had his partner Michael pass away years ago who was very fond of animals and lived above the apartment that Wooster lived in with his mama 'Sarah' before she passed. I wonder if that's who he's with in Spirit sometimes, I love that he had friends waiting for him on the other side when he crossed. I'm so glad to know he's out of pain and he likes to accompany me even out of the house! That's so cool! I also think I recognize the three mother figure spirits and that's such a good feeling."*

Wooster Moved On
Paul was concerned that Wooster may not have moved on and decided to stay with him as a ghost. He asked if Wooster is attached to the building or to him. But Wooster assured me he crossed over and confirmed it by conveying the details of spirits with him.

Only earthbound ghosts choose to fix themselves to a structure. But as a spirit who has crossed over, Wooster can visit Paul anywhere, anytime and anywhere. Paul was relieved to know did not stay behind and attach himself to the building. He was also appreciative of the clarification on the difference between earthbound ghosts and spirits who crossed into the light.

Wooster is "Number One"
Wooster also wanted to convey a number that has a personal significance to him. I wrote Paul, "He's talking about the

number 1. Perhaps someone told him he's 'number 1' or he was the first at something. The numeral one could also signify a day, month (January), or time - that could indicate a birthday, anniversary, passing or adoption day, month, or time. Whenever you see '111' or '1111' (like on the clock) you'll know he's around."

Paul confirmed that "one" was indeed his number. Paul wrote, *"For the 'number 1,' we used to ALWAYS say he was the most beautiful cat in the galaxy, all the time. I catch myself saying that whenever I say or think his name and I'm glad he still knows and remembers he's my "number one." And we did get him in January of 2013. Just thank you so much for your messages. I'll be on the lookout for those numbers too."*

Already Found a Cat to Adopt
Finally, Wooster told me about Paul's new cat! I wrote, "Wooster says he already led you to another black cat who resembled him but was heavier. LOL. He was very aware of his weight and shape. - As if he were on a special diet."

Paul had indeed adopted another cat after Wooster passed, and he wrote, *"You were absolutely correct on Wooster leading us to another cat that resembles him, a really cute and chunky guy named 'Edgar.' That is amazing you got that because they really do look alike! And Wooster was a bigger guy, but Edgar is definitely a chunky cat and he's been on a special diet since we've had him (he's been as large at 24 pounds to right now at 17.50 pounds but when we got him, he was exactly 20 pounds - in fact, his adoption picture was him on a scale, LOL!). We adore him and he is such a love bug."*

***

Paul's email with confirmations of Wooster's messages is the reason I do what I do. He wrote, *"Thank you so much for your message and sending your reading this evening! It was such a cool surprise to receive this early and well worth the wait.*

Wooster's reading was spot on, incredibly so! I had to re-read it a few times to really let that sink in and once again, thank you for your thoroughness and details. It felt like an email from a friend, and I really appreciate the time you took as I know you're quite busy and much in demand (I follow you on Facebook)."

Like Po's dad earlier in this book, Wooster's dad may honor Wooster's memory through art or music. There are so many ways to honor our cats in spirit, so find what is best for you.

***

Wooster's reading is a good example of how much our cats take in when they are with us in the physical and how much they can share from the other side. When you think your cat isn't listening or paying attention, he/she really is making mental notes!

###

Paul Straitjacket (Paul Ybarra) is a Los Angeles based artist and musician best known for his 2014 album "In the Stillness of Remembering: Words and Music by Stevie Nicks (with John Boswell)." Paul's art has gained moderate attention but mostly notoriety in its absurdity and creativity, combining gay, disco, and cultural icons as mythological and metaphysical archetypes. In 2020 his set of the Tarot's Major Arcana represented each by famous and former famous celebrities drew curious interest and attention; Paul's work is all hand drawn with pencil, ink and watercolor. Visit Paul at: www.straitjackettarot.com

###

Chapter 32
The Reincarnation Question

People who lose their pets sometimes want to know if their pet will reincarnate as another pet during their lifetime. In my experience, the answer is "usually, no." Instead, our pets wait for us on the other side to make our transition easier.

As I was finishing my Pets 3 book, I received an email from a reader of one of my other Pets books. She had a question about reincarnation.

She had been to other mediums, and a few told her that if she adopted another dog, her deceased dog's spirit would quickly reincarnate into that other dog. That is not my experience, and I think it's misleading. Here's why.

My belief that pets don't come back to us in **this** physical lifetime is based on the thousands of pets I've communicated with in spirit. I'm not saying they don't reincarnate. *They certainly do come back*. But in my experience, they come back with us in our next lifetime. Until then, they usually wait for us in the light until it's our time and help us cross over.

I understand that in our grief, we so desperately want to see our pets again, but expecting them to quickly come back in another form seems a lot to ask.

Another medium may receive a different message from a pet, which is entirely possible, as everyone and every pet is different. Perhaps a particular pet may be in a hurry to come back to the physical while a person is still alive, but it is highly likely the pet would not retain the memory of their past life.

In addition, it doesn't make sense to me for pets to reincarnate in our lifetime, because pets in spirit know they can still be around us in their afterlife (energy) form. They know they can give us signs to confirm they are around. From spirit, they help teach our new pets learn some of their habits. They also ask human spirits on the other side for assistance to convey their messages.

So, why don't our pets reincarnate quickly?
Pets don't usually reincarnate quickly because they are connected to us in every lifetime. That means that when we pass, our pets will come back when we do, so we'll all be together in the next lifetime.

Why do they wait for us?
Pets wait for us in the afterlife to make our transition to the afterlife easier. They are an entity we can look forward to seeing in the light when it is our time to transition.

When my mom passed in December 2013, my dad's spirit showed up in mom's hospital room and he was holding the spirit of our family toy poodle, Gigi. Gigi passed 20 years before in 1993 and was my mother's heart dog (that is, her most special dog).

Before mom passed, she lay in a coma, but I know she could hear my voice when I spoke to her. When I told my mom that Gigi's spirit was with my dad, that was all she needed to hear. Mom crossed over a couple of hours later.

Some of our pets in spirit even act as spirit guides for us. That means that they guide us in decisions and protect us. As you have read in earlier chapters, our pets in spirit lead us to our next pet they want us to adopt.

In terms of mediums and their abilities, not everyone is the same. Further, no one here has all the answers. We can only convey what spirits tells us. We don't know the answers and won't until we are on the other side.

I personally don't think it's helpful to tell someone their pet reincarnates immediately and finds their pet parent again in this lifetime. I think it gives people a false hope that their cat or cat has suddenly *come back to life in a different form*. It also leads to expectations that their new pet will remember everything from their previous life, and they likely won't. Otherwise, we would remember every one of our past lives.

(Photo: My favorite photo of my Dolly as a puppy. Credit: R. Gutro)

I guess I could understand a medium saying that quick reincarnation occurs, perhaps to try and comfort someone in their grief. However, I would never mislead anyone in thinking that - because it's not my experience with the thousands of animals who have communicated with me.

I hoped my puppy Buzz would come back, but of course he did not. Instead, he is one of my spirit guides that enables me to communicate with animals on the other side. So, there's no right answer, and I can only relate my experiences.

Anything can happen, of course. Although I take comfort in knowing that all my dogs in spirit will be waiting for me on the other side with tails wagging to greet me, as I'm confident your cats will be waiting for you. Hopefully, the imagery of this reunion will provide you some comfort.

###

Conclusion: A Cat's Love Lives Forever

Our cats remember what we have done with them during their lifetime with us and they acknowledge those things from the other side. They treasure the memories we created together and the bonds we developed. They share events, likes, and dislikes with me so their parents can confirm their identities.

The resounding messages I receive over and over are: "thank you," "I love you," and "I'm pain-free now."

They know it takes great courage for us as parents to make that final choice and allow them to cross over and pass out of pain. They often say to their pet parents, "Please don't feel guilty. You did it out of unselfish love." Cats read our emotions, even at the end of their lives when they may be fading. They understand a lot more than we think they do.

For the cats who come to us later in their lives or post-kittenhood, they will be linked to us in the afterlife. The same goes for cats who came from broken homes or abusive situations. They will be bonded to the most recent pet parent (you) and not the people who abused or neglected them. It's love that binds us together.

If a cat comes to you after their pet parent passes, they will be connected to both of you on the other side. Love is like an invisible tether and a spiderweb connecting to many places (people and pets in this instance).

Because cats have intelligence on many levels, they will always have the ability to communicate from the other side. Sometimes they even recruit a human spirit on the other side to help them send messages in the physical world. It doesn't have to be a human they physically met before. One example of a human spirit's help is typing a *"Love you"* message mysteriously on your cell phone (it's happened).

The messages cats in the afterlife have shared with me and their pet parents are proof that their love binds us together forever.

Now that you've read the book, my hope is that you can better cope with their physical loss, by knowing your cat or cats are around in spirit.

A Final Note: Honoring Your Cat
If you want to honor the memory of your beloved cat, you could rescue another cat who is in desperately in need of a home (if you are ready). Pets who pass often tell me a good way to honor their memory is to help another. You may also volunteer at a shelter, or donate to a rescue in your pet's memory.

If your friends want to provide comfort to you during your time of grief ask them to donate to an animal rescue in your pet's name. That's a wonderful way to memorialize your pet and another way to make your pet's spirit smile from the other side.

I have several dogs in spirit, and I've asked them for help with our living dogs and they've provided it. You can do the same with your cats in spirit.

Each night I look at photos of my dogs who have passed and I tell them I love them, and I say goodnight. I know they hear me, as your cats in spirit can hear you.

Our lives have been enriched by the unconditional love of our cats and will continue to be as they love us from spirit.

Wishing you comfort and peace.

Rob Gutro

To read more about ghosts and spirits, pets or people, visit my blog at: *www.robgutro.com or www.petspirits.com*

###

With Appreciation

This book would not have been possible without the assistance, time, personal stories and edits from the people who agreed to share their stories about their special feline family members.

I am grateful to my friend Kristin Young who provided a chapter on methods to help cope you with the grief resulting from the passing of our pets.

I am grateful to Getcovers.com for the amazing cover they created that features images of Coco, Fudge and Gracie whose stories are featured in this book.

I am honored to include the personal stories from so many wonderful people that I've met as a result of my first four volumes of *Pets and the Afterlife*. I hope that by sharing their stories, it has given them comfort to know that their beloved family member will be immortalized in print, and their stories have given others comfort and understanding that their pets are also waiting for them and around them from time to time.

If you know of a rescue that would like to have me speak as a fundraiser, tell them about me and have them contact me at Rgutro@gmail.com. I schedule talks on the weekends and can even do them via Facebook Live or Zoom as fundraisers.

###

Bibliography

All photos of cats in each chapter were provided by their pet parents. All pet parents' full names have been left off for privacy reasons.

Chapter 5: Q&A About People and Pets who Grieve
It's heartbreaking': Killer whale continues carrying dead calf for 'unprecedented' length of mourning
By Ayana Archie and Jay Croft, CNN
Updated 2:47 PM EDT, Sat August 11, 2018
https://www.cnn.com/2018/08/10/us/orca-whale-still-carrying-dead-baby-trnd/index.html

Chapter 9: Time, Transition and Signs
Coren, Stanley; The Intelligence of Dogs; 2006, Pocket Books, Simon & Schuster, UK.

Coren, Stanley; How Dogs Think, 2004, Free Press a division of Simon and Schuster, New York, N.Y.

Grandin, Temple; Animals in Translation; 2006; Harcourt, Orlando, Fla.

Takagi, S., Saito, A., Arahori, M. *et al.* Cats learn the names of their friend cats in their daily lives. *Sci Rep* **12,** 6155 (2022). https://doi.org/10.1038/s41598-022-10261-5
https://www.nature.com/articles/s41598-022-10261-5

About the Author

(Photo: Rob with Dolly, Franklin, and Tyler. Credit: Tom W.)

Rob considers himself to be an average guy, who just happens to be able to hear, feel, sense, and communicate with Earth-bound ghosts and spirits who have passed on. He is a medium and paranormal investigator on the Inspired Ghost Tracking team in the state of Maryland, U.S.A.

When not communicating with the dead, Rob communicates with the living. He's a meteorologist by trade who enjoys talking about weather at any time. Rob worked as a radio broadcast meteorologist at the Weather Channel. He has almost 20 years of on-air radio broadcasting experience.

Rob enjoys taking ghost walks in various cities and visiting historic houses and sites to see who is still lingering behind and encourages them to move into the light to find peace.

Rob and his husband are dog parents and volunteers with Dachshund and Weimaraner dog rescues in their spare time. They have fostered and transported many dogs, worked with shelters, rescue coordinators and veterinarians to save the lives of dogs.

He is an avid reader and collector of comic books and has always loved the mysterious heroes. Since he was a boy, one of his favorite superheroes has always been the ghostly avenger created in the 1940s called "The Spectre."

Website/Blog: www.robgutro.com or www.petspirits.com or

Facebook pages:
https://www.facebook.com/RobGutroAuthorMedium
https://www.facebook.com/ghostsandspirits.insightsfromame dium

Instagram: https://www.instagram.com/robgutro_author/

Amazon Author Page: amazon.com/author/robgutro

YouTube: https://plus.google.com/collection/ok7wh

Email: Rgutro@gmail.com

Other pet titles from Rob Gutro

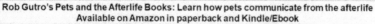

Pets and the Afterlife 1, 2 and 3

The love we share with our pets never dies, and the author proves our pets do communicate with us from the other side. In Rob's 3 best-selling books, learn how dogs, cats, horses, and some birds have the intelligence and ability to send signs to the living after they pass.

Take comfort in knowing our pets are around us from time to time and recognize the signs they give. Learn how they wait for us when it's our time, what a pet's ashes can do, and the difference between ghosts and spirits. Learn how and why living pets can sense entities. In book 1, one of the author's dogs works a ghost investigation and solves a mystery.

Read how spirits of the author's dogs and dogs from three other mediums communicated with them from the other side. Available in paperback and E-book on Amazon.com.

Pets and the Afterlife 3 won Book Authority's International Book Award for one of the "Best Books on Grief" for 2021 and 2022, and debuted on Amazon at the number 1 spot.

Other titles from Rob Gutro

Rob's Books are available in paperback and E-Book on www.Amazon.com. They include:
Case Files of Inspired Ghost Tracking
Kindred Spirits
Ghosts of England on a Medium's Vacation
Ghosts of the Bird Cage Theatre on a Medium's Vacation
Pets and the Afterlife
Pets and the Afterlife 2
Pets and the Afterlife 3
Lessons Learned from Talking to the Dead
Ghosts and Spirits Explained

Printed in Great Britain
by Amazon